veera välimäki

Color Wheel Knits

[Knits for Hand Dyed Yarns]

Co-Operative Press

color wheel knits

Color Wheel Knits

[Knits for Hand Dyed Yarns]

veera välimäki

Cooperative Press

Contents

Color play

– introduction to the world of hand dyed yarns

Hand dyed yarn is now probably more popular than ever. Who wouldn't love to look at, touch and knit with handpainted yarn? What I love most about hand dyed yarn is the vivid and luminous quality of color in these precious skeins. The depth of color in a single hand dyed skein is almost impossible to put into words. What knitter wouldn't love a few skeins of hand dyed yarn – all different and all wonderful in their own way! The variety of hand dyed yarn today is amazing, there are plenty of wonderful dyers to be found.

For this book, I have divided the color wheel into four color groups and chosen a few patterns for each color group. The designs are mostly simple with modern details and techniques to highlight each color and the endless possibilities of the different yarns. The design selection varies from quick mittens to longer projects such as sweaters for men or lightweight tunics for women.

WONDERS OF WOOL

In knitting, I strongly prefer wool and other natural fibers such as silk, and that preference shows in the yarns I've chosen for this book. Wool is warm and it breathes. It is both hard-wearing and lightweight at the same time. Also, wool is resistant to dirt, wear and tear. Simply put, wool is extremely versatile. The different types of wool give you never-ending possibilities to choose from: all the way from durable Blue-faced Leicester to lightweight merino. For a dyer, wool is a good choice because it absorbs color easier than many plant-based fibers do.

Wool is a wonderful and sustainable material, whose production doesn't strain the environment too much. To avoid unnecessary strain to nature and the animals and other issues that can occur with factory farming and in the mass production of wool, choose organically produced wool whenever possible.

SECRETS OF DYEING

It's said that dyeing is almost as old as the practice of fabric making. Colors in the muddy range of reds and browns are the first colors found in a number of ancient textile sites ranging from the Neolithic to the Bronze Age across Egypt, Mesopotamia and Europe. Next followed blues and then yellows, with green appearing somewhat later. Based on the colors of surviving textile fragments and the evidence of actual dyestuffs found in archaeological sites, reds, blues, and yellows from plant sources were in common use already by the Iron Age and even by the late Bronze Age.

Natural dyeing was long a part of our common know-how. The invention of synthetic dyes made this skill unnecessary to many, and natural dyeing was partially forgotten for a while. Now the tradition has been updated to modern knowledge.

In this book I have used both synthetically and naturally dyed yarns. There are so many wonderful dyers to be found all over the world. I wanted to highlight a few of my personal favorites, from Finland to Australia. The different spectrums created by these highly skilled artists are something truly amazing. The depth of color seen in many hand dyed skeins simply takes your breath away and the un-repeatable and ever-changing nature is captivating.

FROM SKEIN TO GARMENT

Sometimes, the individual quality we love in these lovingly painted or dyed skeins can be extremely frustrating when knitting. The beautiful and harmonious colors in skein can turn into a big mess of hues when knitted; the colors can create large irregular areas, i.e. pool, form diagonal columns or stripe. First you should examine the skein closely, even open it up on a table to fully see the color changes. Since color pooling is relatively unpredictable, I also strongly recommend that you work a large swatch get a good sense of the particular coloway of the skein.

You can ease up the blending of different hues in many different ways. The simplest technique is to try a different gauge in your knitting – you can be astonished how the gauge affects your fabric. Also different stitch patterns, everything from basic garter stitch to more complex mixture of slipped stitches, will make the color changes less visible. If the color changes happen to be very short, changing often, you can also try working with double strands.

In larger garments (like sweaters and shawls), it's extremely important to try to match up the skeins as closely as possible, and still some differences, or individuality, will most likely remain from skein to skein. Striping is also a way to even out variegated colorways, then work alternating two different skeins working two rows with each skein. When knitting with semi-solid yarn, those skeins that have only slight tonal variation and appear as almost one color, you can alternate skeins only for an inch before skein change.

To see the changes unfold is also an enjoyable part of knitting when working with handpainted yarn. I encourage you to let the yarn show the way!

COLOR WHEEL KNITS

All the designs in this book are seamless and they often feature different types of short rows to achieve the best possible fit. The knitting vocabulary is a mixture of explicitness and short phrasing.

The designs try to give all the needed space for the yarn, that's why I've tried to keep things simple. I'm particu-larly drawn to basic stitch patterns such as garter stitch and Stockinette stitch, to let the yarn do most of the effect. Hopefully the result is something modern and appealing.

HOPE YOU ENJOY THIS JOURNEY INTO THE WORLD OF HAND DYED YARN!

—*veera*

Blue
like the sky
without rain

Blue and Green

Nature is filled with blue and green hues - blue in the sky and the ocean, green in vegetation. Often these colors are associated with calmness, concentration and stability. Studies show that blue is reported to be the favorite color of people universally. As it appears in abundance all over the world, may help explain its popularity.

IN EUROPE, blue dyes were long rare – blue was a color of luxury. Blue gained a prestigious status in European art in the Middle Ages when artists learned how to produce vivid blue hues from ultramarine, which was a pigment in a stone called lapis lazuli. Ultramarine was a very expensive pigment, more costly than gold. In paintings, it was reserved for the mantel of Virgin Mary – not long after, monarchs decided that blue or bluish purple should be the color of the their robes too. Blue dye was also expensive, and only the royal and the rich could afford it. In the Middle Ages, Europeans produced their blue dye from woad, a native plant in south-eastern Europe.

Globally, however, the most important source of natural blue dye was the indigo plant, which had been used for dyeing in warmer climates since ancient times. The most important producer of indigo was India. From the late 18th century onwards blue was no longer reserved for the elites: as cotton plantations increased, denim was discovered to be a durable material suitable for hard physical work. Denim was traditionally dyed with natural indigo due to its practicality: it was widely available, durable and dark enough to hide stains.

THE COLOR GREEN is likewise often considered relaxing; since ancient times, it has been widely believed that green is beneficial and soothing for the eye.

Even though green is such a dominant color in vegetation, it is surprising that nature does not provide plants or minerals that could be used in the production of really bright green dyes . Before the discovery of synthetic green dye in the 19th century, the green color in textiles was often obtained by dyeing blue fabric with yellow.

Concrete

Concrete is an easy-to-wear, long pullover with a large, warming cowl. Garter stitch rib paired with rustic wool makes this little piece a joy to knit, especially in this vivid and perfectly named blue colorway — "A whale's song."

Materials

Yarns

3 (4, 4, 5, 5, 5) skeins of Louhitar by Knitlob's Lair (100% wool, 267 yds [244 m] /100 g). Approx. 800 (880, 980, 1100, 1200, 1280) yards [730 (800, 900, 1000, 1100, 1170) meters] of sport weight yarn. Sample was knit in the colorway Valaan Laulu and in size small.

Needles

US 6 [4 mm] and US 4 [3.5 mm] circular needles, 24″ [60 cm] long, and dpns. Adjust needle size if necessary to obtain the correct gauge.

Notions

Tapestry needle, stitch markers, stitch holders/waste yarn and blocking aids.

Sizing

XS (S, M, L, XL, XXL)

Finished chest circumference: 30 (34, 38, 42, 46, 50)″ [75 (85, 95, 105, 115, 125) cm]. The pullover is intended to be worn with zero to a small amount of positive ease.

Gauge

20 sts and 28 rows = 4″ [10 cm] in garter stitch rib using larger needles.

Finished measurements

28 (28½, 29, 29, 30, 31)″
[70 (71, 73, 73, 75, 76) cm]

10½ (11½, 12½, 13½, 14, 16)″
[27 (29, 31, 34, 36, 40) cm]

8 (8¼, 8¾, 9¼, 9½, 10)″
[19 (20, 21, 22, 23, 25) cm]

17 (17, 18, 18, 19, 19)″
[44 (44, 46, 46, 48, 48) cm]

30 (34, 38, 42, 46, 50)″
[75 (85, 95, 105, 115, 125) cm]

Stitch patterns

GARTER STITCH RIB

In the round: alternate knit rounds and *k1, p1;
–rounds.

Back and forth: *k on RS, *k1, p1; repeat from * to
end on WS.

TWISTED RIB

In the round: *k1 tbl, p1; repeat from * to end of
round.

Collar

Using smaller circular needle CO 138 (142, 146, 146, 150, 154) sts. Pm to indicate the beginning of the round and join carefully not twisting your stitches. Work in twisted ribbing until the piece measures 2″ [5 cm]. Change to larger circular needle and continue in garter st rib. Pm for side: work 69 (71, 73, 73, 75, 77) sts in garter st rib, pm, work to end in garter st rib. When the collar measures 8″ [20 cm] begin collar decreases.

DECREASE ROUND: work 4 sts in garter st rib, ssk, work in garter st rib until 6 sts before m remain, k2tog, work to marker in garter st rib, work 5 sts in garter st rib, ssk, work in garter st rib until 7 sts before m remain, k2tog, work to end in garter st rib.

Repeat the decrease round every 8th round for 5 more times [*24 sts decreased; 114 (118, 122, 122, 126, 130) sts on the needle*]. *Note: Work the two stitches next to decrease point similarly after each odd decrease round; after even number of decreases the garter stitch rib will be continuous again.* Work even in garter st rib until collar measures 18″ [35 cm], ending with *k1, p1 -round.

Yoke

Continue in garter st rib and begin the yoke increases and short rows as follows. *Note: make sure you have a knit stitch on marker side of each raglan increase point.*

ROW 1 (RS, setup row): k 6 (6, 4, 4, 2, 2), m1R, k 3 (2, 3, 2, 3, 3), pm (left back raglan), k 2 (3, 2, 3, 2, 2), m1L, k 35 (37, 43, 43, 49, 51), m1R, k 2 (3, 2, 3, 2, 2), pm (right back raglan), k 3 (2, 3, 2, 3, 3), m1L, k 12 (12, 8, 8, 4, 4) (removing side m), m1R, k 3 (2, 3, 2, 3, 3), pm (right front raglan), k 2 (3, 2, 3, 2, 2), m1L, k2, turn work.

ROW 2 (WS, setup row): yo, *work to m in garter st rib (k1, p1 -row; *note: all the increased sts are now worked as purl stitches as are the ones closer to raglan markers*); repeat twice from *, work to beg of rnd marker in garter st rib, sm, p 6 (6, 4, 4, 2, 2), m1R (purl), p 3 (2, 3, 2, 3, 3), pm (left front raglan), p 2 (3, 2, 3, 2, 2), m1L (purl), p2, turn work.

ROW 3 (RS): yo, work to m in garter st rib (k1, p1, -row), sm, work to beg of rnd marker in garter st rib, sm, k until 3 (2, 3, 2, 3, 3) sts before m remain, m1R, k to m, sm, k 2 (3, 2, 3, 2, 2), m1L, k until 2 (3, 2, 3, 2, 2) sts before m remain, m1R, k to m, sm, k 3 (2, 3, 2, 3, 3), m1L, k until 3 (2, 3, 2, 3, 3) sts before m remain, m1R, k to m, sm, k 2 (3, 2, 3, 2, 2), m1L, k to previous yo, k2tog the yo with the next st, k1, turn work.

ROW 4 (WS): yo, *work to m in garter st rib (k1, p1 -row), sm; repeat twice from *, work to beg of rnd marker in garter st rib, sm, p until 3 (2, 3, 2, 3, 3) sts before m remain, m1R (purl), p to m, sm, p 2 (3, 2, 3, 2, 2), m1L (purl), p to previous yo, ssp the yo with the next st, p1, turn work.

Work rows 3 and 4 — 4 (4, 5, 6, 7, 8) times more. Work to end of round as follows: yo, work to m in garter st rib (k1, p1, -row), sm, work to beg of rnd marker in garter st rib.

Continue in the round, working increases every second round (knit round). *Note: Work the two stitches next to decrease point similarly after each odd decrease round; after even number of decreases the garter stitch rib will be continuous again. On first time working row 5, pick up the last yarn-overs (k2tog the first yo with the next st and ssk the second with previous st).*

ROUND 5 (increase round, knit round): sm (beg of rnd), k until 3 (2, 3, 2, 3, 3) sts before m remain, m1R, k to m, sm, k 2 (3, 2, 3, 2, 2), m1L, k until 2 (3, 2, 3, 2, 2) sts before m remain, m1R, k to m, sm, k 3 (2, 3, 2, 3, 3), m1L, k until 3 (2, 3, 2, 3, 3) sts before m remain, m1R, k to m, sm, k 2 (3, 2, 3, 2, 2), m1L, k until 2 (3, 2, 3, 2, 2) sts before m remain, m1R, k to m, sm, k 3 (2, 3, 2, 3, 3), m1L, k to beg of rnd marker.

ROUND 6: *sm, work to m in garter st rib; repeat four times from *.

Work rounds 5 and 6 – 11 (14, 16, 19, 21, 24) times more. After all increase rounds you have 258 (286, 314, 346, 374, 410) sts on needle.

DIVIDE FOR BODY AND SLEEVES

Remove marker, work to next m and place those lastly worked stitches on holder for sleeve, remove m, work to next m, sm, work to m and place those lastly worked stitches on another holder/waste yarn for second sleeve, remove m, work to m, sm, work to end and place those stitches on first holder/waste yarn for sleeve.

You have now 54 (58, 62, 68, 72, 80) sts on each holder for sleeves and 150 (170, 190, 210, 234, 250) sts on the needle for the body.

Body

Continue even, working garter stitch rib. When the body measures 2½″ [7 cm] from underarm, begin waist shaping.

DECREASE ROUND (knit round): sm, k6, ssk, k until 8 sts before m remain, k2tog, k to m, sm, k5, ssk, k until 7 sts before m remain, k2tog, k to end.

Repeat the decrease row three more times on every 6th round *(16 sts decreased; 134 (154, 174, 194, 218, 234) sts remain)*. Work even additional 2″ [5 cm].

INCREASE ROUND (knit round): sm, k7, m1R, k until 7 sts before m remain, m1L, k to m, sm, k6, m1R, k until 6 sts before m remain, m1L, k to end.

Repeat the increase row 7 more times on every 6th round *(32 sts increased; 166 (186, 206, 226, 246, 266) sts on needle)*. Continue even in garter st rib until the body measures 15 (15, 16, 16, 17, 17)″ [40 (40, 42, 42, 44, 44) cm] from underarm. Change to smaller circular needle and work 2″ [5 cm] in twisted rib. BO sts loosely in ribbing.

Sleeves

Note: You can pick a few extra stitches from the underarm for all sizes to prevent hole – or sew the gap while finishing the garment. Decrease these extra picked up stitches on next possible round.

Place the 54 (58, 62, 68, 72, 80) sts of sleeve from holder on larger dpns. Pm to indicate beginning of the round and join yarn. Work even in garter st rib until the sleeve measures 1″ [2.5 cm] from underarm. Change to smaller dpns and work 2″ [5 cm] in twisted rib. BO sts loosely in ribbing.

Finishing

Weave in all yarn ends. Wet block the pullover to measurements.

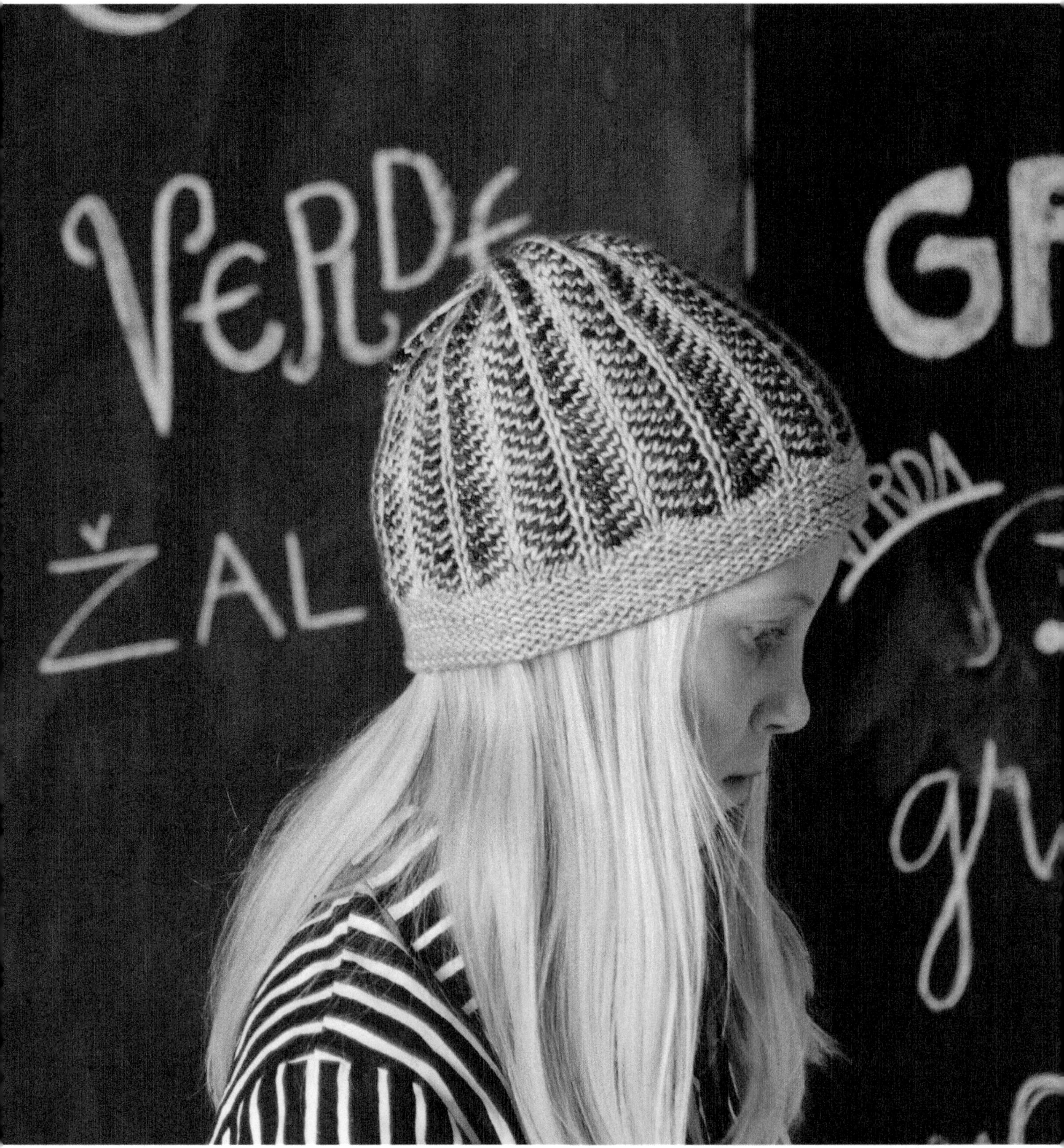
VERDE
ŽAL

Spruce

Spruce is a simple beanie with lovely striped chevron pattern. It looks sharp and striking, but is really easy to knit. Not to mention the endless possibilities for color combinations.

Materials

Yarn

2 skeins of Tosh Sport by Madelinetosh (100% Superwash Merino, 270 yds [247 m]/ skein). Approx. 200 yards [180 meters] of heavy sport weight yarn, both colors included. Sample was knit in the colorways Smokestack (MC) and Cousteau (CC); in kids size.

Needles

US 6 [4 mm] dpns and circular needles 16" [40 cm] long. Adjust needle size if necessary to obtain the correct gauge.

Notions

Tapestry needle, stitch markers, stitch holders/ waste yarn and blocking aids.

Sizing

Kids (Teens, Adults)

Finished brim circumference, unstretched: 14½ (16½, 18)" [36 (40; 45) cm].

Gauge

22 sts and 30 rows = 4" [10 cm] in chevron pattern.

Brim

Using circular needle and MC, CO 80 (90, 100) sts. Join in the round carefully not twisting your stitches and pm for beg of rnd. Work in garter st (alternate k and p rounds), but work the first st of round in St st (k every round), until the brim measures 1¼″ [3 cm]. Increase for the body on last knit round: *k 4 (4, 5), m1, k 4 (5, 5); repeat from * to end of round [*20 sts increased; 100 (110, 120) sts on needle*].

Chevron pattern

Change to chevron pattern. *Note: Remember to twist yarn at color changes to avoid weaving in many yarn ends.*

ROUND 1 (MC): *k1, k2tog, k2, m1R, k1, m1L, k2, ssk; repeat from * to end of round.

ROUND 2 (CC): *slip 1, k 4; repeat from * to end of round.

Repeat rounds 1 and 2 for chevron pattern. Continue as established until the beanie measures 6 (7, 8)″ [15 (18, 20) cm].

BEGIN DECREASES

Note: change to dpns when necessary.

ROUND 3 (MC, decrease rnd): *k1, k2tog, k to next slipped st, k1, k until 2 sts before next slipped st remain, ssk; repeat from * to end of round.

ROUND 4 (CC): *slip 1, k 3; repeat from * to end of round.

ROUND 5 (MC): *k1, k2tog, k1, m1R, k1, m1L, k1, ssk; repeat from * to end of round.

ROUND 6 (CC): *slip 1, k 3; repeat from * to end of round.

Repeat rounds 5 and 6 once more.

ROUND 7 (MC, decrease rnd): *k1, k2tog, k to next slipped st, k1, k until 2 sts before next slipped st remain, ssk; repeat from * to end of round.

ROUND 8 (CC): *slip 1, k2; repeat from * to end of round.

ROUND 9 (MC): *k1, k2tog, m1R, k1, m1L, ssk; repeat from * to end of round.

ROUND 10 (CC): *slip 1, k2; repeat from * to end of round.

Repeat rounds 9 and 10 once more. Continue in MC only alternating k2tog-rounds (*k2tog; repeat to end of round) and St st rounds. When 10 sts remain, cut yarn and thread through the remaining stitches twice for closure.

Finishing

Weave in all yarn ends. Block the beanie to measurements using your preferred method.

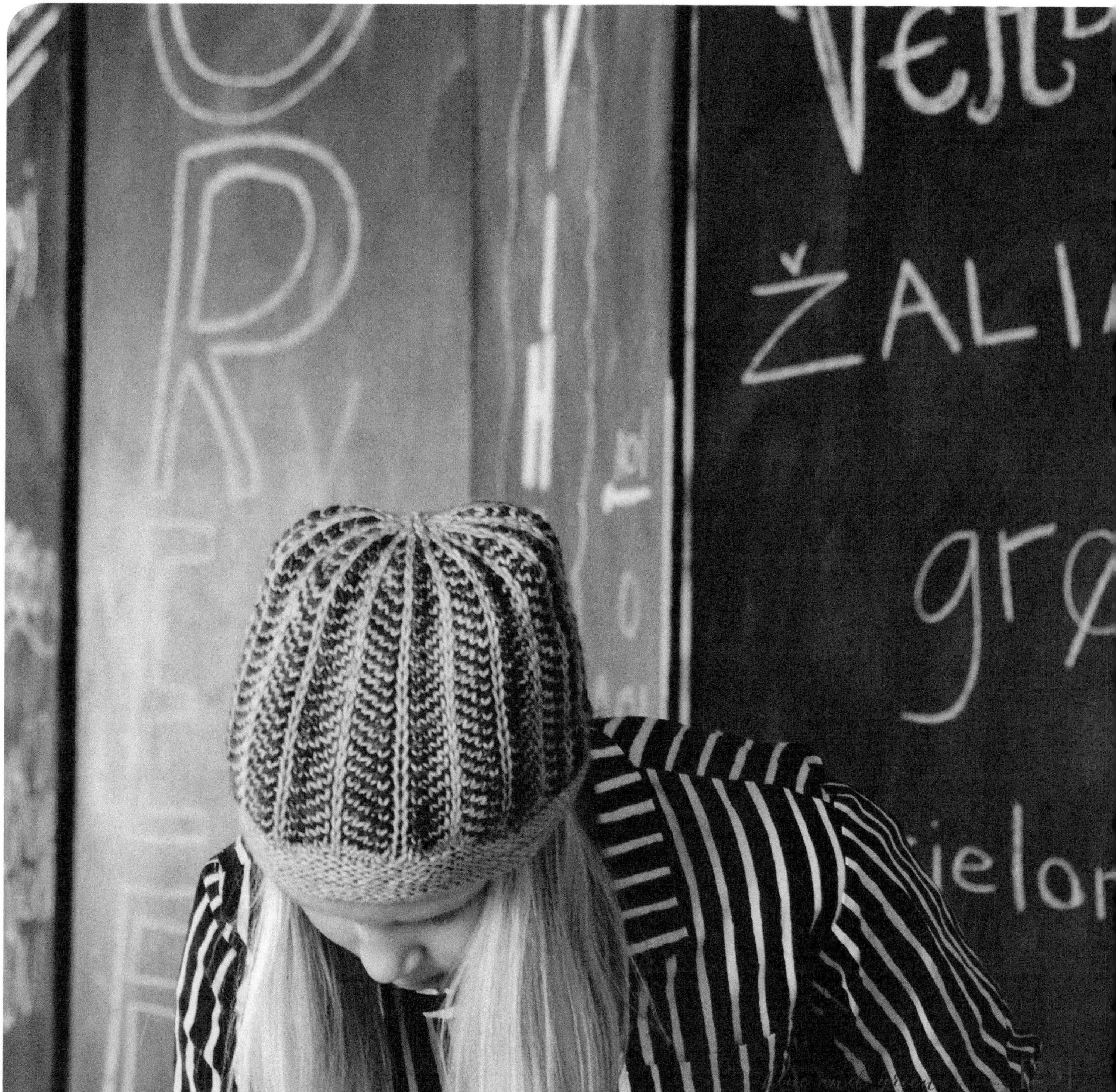

Tin Soldier

Tin Soldier is a cardigan for playful days. Simple garter stitch is broken with Stockinette columns in both the sleeves and in the body. Finalize the cardigan with your favourite buttons and it will be a cardigan your kids want to wear every day!

Materials

Yarn

2 (3, 3, 3, 4, 4) skeins of BFL DK by Lioness Arts (100% wool; 245 yds [224 m] per 100 g). Approx. 480 (570, 680, 765, 850, 940) yards [440 (520, 620, 700, 780, 860) meters] of DK weight yarn. Sample was knit in the colorways Space and in size 6.

Needles

US 6 [4 mm] circular needles; 24″ [60 cm] long, and dpns. Adjust needle size if necessary to obtain the correct gauge.

Notions

Six 1¼″ [3 cm] buttons, stitch markers, tapestry needle, blocking aids.

Sizing

2 (4, 6, 8, 10, 12) Years

Finished chest circumference: 23 (25½, 27, 29, 30½, 32)″ [58 (64, 68, 73, 76, 80) cm] buttoned.

Gauge

20 sts and 32 rows = 4″ [10 cm] in garter stitch.

Finished measurements

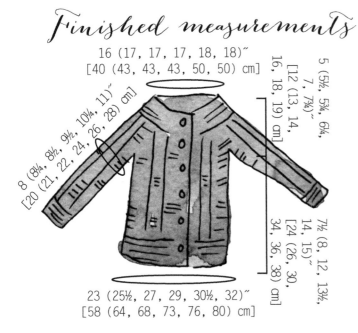

16 (17, 17, 17, 18, 18)″
[40 (43, 43, 43, 50, 50) cm]

5 (5½, 5¾, 6¼, 7, 7¾)″ [12 (13, 14, 16, 18, 19) cm]

8 (8¼, 8½, 9½, 10¼, 11)″ [20 (21, 22, 24, 26, 28) cm]

7¾ (8, 12, 13¾, 14, 15)″ [24 (26, 30, 34, 36, 38) cm]

23 (25½, 27, 29, 30½, 32)″
[58 (64, 68, 73, 76, 80) cm]

Collar

Using circ needle, CO 90 (96, 96, 96, 100, 100) sts. Work back and forth in garter st until the piece measures 1″ [2.5 cm]. Work first buttonhole on next row (RS): k 5, ssk, yo, k to end. On next RS row increase for the neck: k 14 (27, 14, 29, 16, 28), *kfb, k2; repeat 19 (11, 21, 11, 21, 13) times more from *, k to end [*110 (108, 118, 108, 122, 114) sts on needle*].

Shape back of the neck with short rows (do not pick up wraps): k until 36 sts remain, W&T, k until 36 sts remain, W&T, *k 2 sts past previous wrapped st, W&T; k 2 sts past previous wrapped st, W&T; repeat from * 4 times more (working both RS and WS short row on each repeat), k to end after last W&T. Continue in garter st until the collar measures 2″ [5 cm] at front. End with a RS row.

Yoke

Continue in garter st and add 12 two-stitch Stockinette columns on first WS row: k 10, p2, k1, p2, k 12 (10, 14, 12, 15, 13), p2, k2, p2, k 12 (10, 14, 11, 15, 13), k2, p2, k1, p2, k 10, p2, k1, p2, k 12 (10, 14, 11, 15, 13), p2, k2, p2, k 12 (10, 14, 12, 15, 13), p2, k1, p2, k to end.

INCREASE ROW (RS): *k to St st column, m1L, k2, m1R; repeat from * 11 times more, k to end. Continue in garter st and 12 Stockinette st columns and repeat the increase row 3 (4, 4, 5, 5, 6) more times every 8th row and work a buttonhole every 1½″ [4 cm]. After last increase row work 3 more rows in garter st and Stockinette stitch columns [*206 (228, 238, 252, 266, 282) sts on the needle*].

DIVIDE FOR BODY AND SLEEVES

(RS): k 32 (34, 36, 39, 40, 42), place the next 40 (42, 46, 48, 52, 56) sts on holder, k 62 (70, 74, 78, 82, 86) sts, place the next 40 (42, 46, 48, 52, 56) sts on holder, k to end.

You have now 40 (42, 46, 48, 52, 56) sts on each holder for sleeves and 126 (138, 146, 156, 162, 170) sts on the needle for the body.

Body

Continue in garter st and 8 two-stitch Stockinette columns of the body and work a buttonhole every 1½″ [4 cm] until you have 6 buttonholes. Work as established until the body measures 5½ (6¼, 8, 9½, 10¼, 11)″ [14 (16, 20, 24, 26, 28) cm]. Continue in garter st until the body measures 9½ (10¼, 12, 13½, 14¼, 15)″ [24 (26, 30, 34, 36, 38) cm]. BO sts loosely on a RS row.

Sleeves

Note: You can pick a few extra stitches from the underarm for all sizes to prevent a hole – or sew the gap while finishing the garment.

Place the 40 (42, 46, 48, 52, 56) sts of sleeve from holder on smaller dpns. Pm to indicate beginning of the round and join yarn to underarm. Work even in garter st and St st columns until the sleeve measures 6 (6½, 8, 9½, 11, 12)″ [15 (17, 20, 24, 28, 30) cm] from underarm. Work 4″ [10 cm] in garter st only (alternate k and p rounds). BO sts loosely.

Finishing

Weave in all yarn ends and sew on buttons. Block the cardigan to measurements using your preferred method.

Green Cables

Green cables is a lovely A-line cardigan with modern and eye-catching details. Simple but large cable panels start from the collar and go all the way to the back of the cardigan.

Materials

Yarn

3 (3, 4, 4, 5, 5) skeins of MCN DK by Lioness Arts (80% merino, 10% nylon, 10% cashmere; 225 yds [205 m] per skein), Approx. 550 (630, 720, 850, 960, 1090) yards [500 (580, 660, 780, 880, 1000) meters] of DK weight yarn. The sample is knit in the colorway "Tree Frog," in size 6 years.

Needles

US 6 [4 mm] and US 8 [5 mm] circular needles, 24″ [60 cm] long, and dpns. Adjust needle size if necessary to obtain the correct gauge.

Notions

Three 1½″ [3 cm] buttons, stitch markers, tapestry needle and blocking aids.

Sizing

2 (4, 6, 8, 10, 12) Years

Finished chest circumference:
23 (25½, 27, 29, 30½, 32)″
[58 (64, 68, 73, 76, 80) cm].

Gauge

18 sts and 26 rows = 4″ [10 cm] in rev St st using larger needle.

Finished measurements

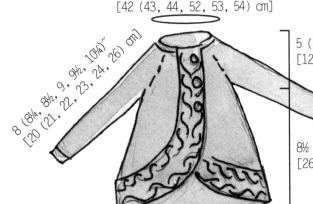

16½ (17, 17¼, 20½, 21, 21½)″
[42 (43, 44, 52, 53, 54) cm]

8 (8¼, 8½, 9, 9½, 10¼)″
[20 (21, 22, 23, 24, 26) cm]

5 (5½, 5¾, 6¼, 7, 7¾)″
[12 (13, 14, 16, 18, 19) cm]

8½ (9, 13, 14½, 15, 16)″
[26 (28, 32, 36, 38, 40) cm]

23 (25½, 27, 29, 30½, 32)″
[58 (64, 68, 73, 76, 80) cm]

Collar

Using smaller circular needle CO 104 (106, 108, 122, 124, 126) sts. Work back and forth in 1×1 ribbing until the piece measures 1″ [2.5 cm]. End with a WS row.

Yoke

Change to larger circular needle and work raglan increases in rev St st and add cables to the fronts.

SETUP ROW (RS): work row 1 of charts A-C, p 0 (0, 0, 3, 3, 3), m1R, p1, pm, p1, m1L, p 8 (8, 8, 10, 10, 10), m1R, p1, pm, p1, m1L, p 24 (26, 28, 32, 34, 36), m1R, p1, pm, p1, m1L, p 8 (8, 8, 10, 10, 10), m1R, p1, pm, p1, m1L, p 0 (0, 0, 3, 3, 3), work row 1 of charts D-F.

SETUP ROW (WS): work row 2 of charts F-D, *k to m, sm; repeat from * three more times, k to front cables (until 28 sts remain), work row 2 of charts C-A.

ROW 1 (RS): work the next row of charts A-C, *p until 1 st before m remains, m1R, p1, sm, p1, m1L; repeat from * three more times, p to front cables (until 28 sts remain), work the next row of charts D-F.

ROW 2 (WS): work the next row of charts F-D, *k to m, sm; repeat from * three more times, k to front cables, work the next row of charts C-A.

Repeat rows 1 and 2 – 11 (12, 13, 14, 15, 16) times more and at the same time work three buttonholes every 2″ [5 cm] (RS): Work the next row of chart A until 1 st of chart remains, yo, k2tog, work to end of row as established [208 (218, 228, 250, 260, 270) sts].

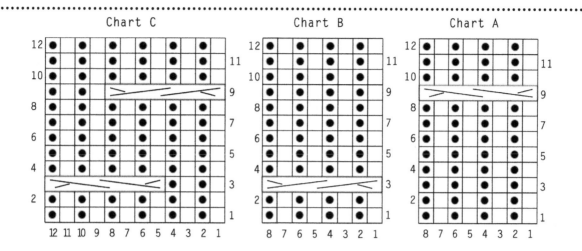

Chart C **Chart B** **Chart A**

Chart key

Note: Read the charts from right to left on RS; left to right on WS.

☐ Work in St st

⬛ Work in rev St st

Slip 4 sts on cable needle and hold at WS of the work, work 4 sts in 1X1 ribbing, work 4 sts from cable needle in 1X1 ribbing.

Slip 4 sts on cable needle and hold at RS of the work, work 4 sts in 1X1 ribbing, work 4 sts from cable needle in 1X1 ribbing.

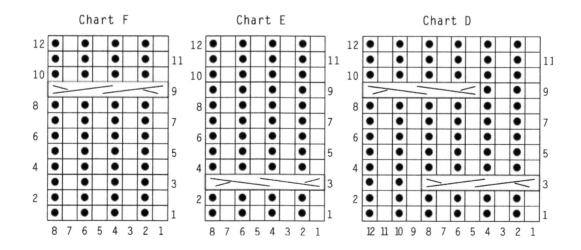

Chart F **Chart E** **Chart D**

Divide for Body and Sleeves

Work the next RS row of charts A-C, *p to m, remove m, place stitches before next marker on holder/waste yarn for sleeve, sm; repeat once from *, work the next row of charts D-F.

You now have 36 (38, 40, 44, 46, 48) sts on each holder for sleeves and 136 (142, 148, 162, 168, 174) sts on the needle for the body.

Body

Work even as established in rev St st and front cables working through charts A-F until the body measures 1 (1, 1½, 1½, 2¼, 2¼)" [2 (2, 4, 4, 6, 6) cm] from underarm and work the 3rd buttonhole if necessary.

Increase row (RS): work the next row of charts A-C, *p until 4 st before m remains, m1R, p to m, sm, p4, m1L; repeat from * once, p to cables (28 sts remain), work the next row of charts D-F.

Work the increase row on every 6th row until the body measures 6¼ (6½, 7, 7, 7½, 8)" [16 (17, 18, 18, 19, 20) cm] from underarm.

Begin short rows to shape the curvy fronts and continue to work the increases as established on every 6th row.

Setup row (RS, work increases if necessary): work the next row of charts A-C, p to m, sm, p to m, sm, p5, turn work.

Setup row (WS): yo, k to m, sm, k to m, sm, k5, turn work.

Row 3 (RS, work increases if necessary): yo, p to m, sm, p to m, sm, p to previous yo, p2tog the yo and the next st, p1, turn work.

Row 4 (WS): yo, k to m, sm, k to m, sm, k to previous yo, ssk the yo and the next st, k1, turn work.

Repeat rows 3 and 4 until 1 st before front cables remain. Work to end of row (RS): p to m sm, p to m, sm, p to previous yo, p2tog the yo and the next st, work the next row of charts D-F. Work 3 whole rows more and pick up the last remaining yo on first WS row (ssk the yo with the next st).

Hem

Left Front and Hem

Continue with the cable stitches of left front only (charts A-C). *Note: If a yarn-over should be worked together with cable stitches on a turning row of the cable, slip the stitches on cable needle first and work the yo together with the next st.*

Rows 5 and 6 (RS and WS): work next row of chart A, turn work; yo, work next row of chart A.

Rows 7 and 8 (RS and WS): work next row of chart A, k2tog the yarn-over and the next st, and at the same time work next row of chart B, turn work; yo, work next row of chart B, work next row of chart A.

Setup rows 9 and 10 *(RS and WS, work only on first repeat of rows 9 and 10)*: work the next row of chart A, work the next row of chart B, k2tog the yarn-over and the next st and at the same time work the next row of chart C, p1, turn work; yo, k1, work the next row of chart C, work the next row of chart B, work the next row of chart A.

Rows 9 and 10 (RS and WS): work next row of chart A, work next row of chart B, k2tog the yarn-over and the next st and at the same time work next row of chart C, p3tog the yo with the previous and next st, turn work; yo, k1, work next row of chart C, work next row of chart B, work next row of chart A.

Repeat short rows 5 to 10 until all curved front sts are worked. Continue short rows working all charts (A-C) on each row —

Rows 11 and 12 (RS and WS): work next row of chart A, work next row of chart B, work next row of chart C, p3tog the yo with the previous and next st, turn work; yo, k1, work next row of chart C, work next row of chart B, work next row of chart A.

Repeat short rows 11 and 12 for an additional 4 (4, 5, 5, 5½, 6¼)″ [10 (10, 12, 12, 14, 16) cm]. Continue as established, but work the cable stitches in 1×1 ribbing until you reach the middle of the back stitches. Place stitches on holder and break yarn.

Right front and hem

Continue with the cable stitches of right front only (charts D-F). Re-attach the yarn to the cable sts of right front with RS facing. *Note: If a yarn-over should be worked together with cable stitches on a turning row of the cable, slip the stitches on cable needle first and work the yo together with the next st.*

Row 13 (RS, setup row): Work next row of charts D-F.

Rows 14 and 15 (WS and RS): Work next row of chart F, turn work; yo, work next row of chart F.

Rows 16 and 17 (WS and RS): work next row of chart F, ssk the yarn-over and the next st and at the same time work next row of chart E, turn work; yo, work next row of chart E, work next row of chart F.

Setup rows 18 and 19 *(WS and RS, work only on first repeat of rows 18 and 19): work next row of chart F, work next row of chart E, ssk the yarn-over and the next st and at the same time work next row of chart D, k1, turn work; yo, p1, work next row of chart D, work next row of chart E, work next row of chart F.*

Rows 18 and 19 (WS and RS): work next row of chart F, work next row of chart E, ssk the yarn-over and the next st and at the same time work next row of chart D, sssk the yo with the previous and next st, turn work; yo, p1, work next row of chart D, work next row of chart E, work next row of chart F.

Repeat short rows 14 to 19 until all curved front sts are worked. Continue short rows working all cables (charts D-F) on each row —

Rows 20 and 21 (WS and RS): work next row of chart F, work next row of chart E, work next row of chart D, sssk the yo with the previous and next st, turn work; yo, p1, work next row of chart D, work next row of chart E, work next row of chart F.

Repeat short rows 20 and 21 for an additional 4 (4, 5, 5, 5½, 6¼)″ [10 (10, 12, 12, 14, 16) cm]. Continue as established, but work the cable stitches in 1×1 ribbing until you reach the middle of the back stitches and the right front stitches. Slip the right hem stitches on a dpn and graft the two edges together. *Note: Graft the first two sts of right edge as a single stitch and the last two of the left edge similarly. That way the ribbing is continuous.*

Sleeves

Note: You can pick a few extra stitches from the underarm for all sizes to prevent hole – or sew the gap while finishing the garment. Decrease these extra picked up stitches on next possible round.

Place the 36 (38, 40, 44, 46, 48) sts of sleeve from holder on larger dpns. Pm to indicate beginning of the round and join yarn. Work even in rev St st until the sleeve measures 2″ [5 cm] from underarm.

DECREASE ROUND: k2, ssk, k until 4 sts remain, k2tog, k to end.

Repeat the decrease round 3 times more every 1½″ [4 cm]. Work even in rev St st until sleeve measures 8½ (9½, 10½, 12, 13, 13½)″ [22 (24, 26, 30, 32, 34) cm] from underarm. Change to smaller dpns and work 1½″ [4 cm] in 1×1 twisted ribbing. BO sts loosely in ribbing.

Finishing

Weave in all yarn ends and sew buttons to left front. Block the cardigan to measurements using your preferred method.

Fine Jacket

FINE JACKET IS IDEAL FOR WORK AND SMARTER DAYS OUT. BEAUTIFUL COLLAR, SET-IN SLEEVES AND LOVELY PLEATS AT FRONT MAKE THIS JACKET BOTH INTERESTING AND MODERN. IT IS WORKED FROM TOP DOWN IN ONE PIECE.

Materials

YARN

5 (6, 6, 7, 8, 8) skeins of Twist by Malabrigo Yarn (100% merino wool, 150 yds [137 m] /100 g). Approx. 750 (830, 900, 1050, 1120, 1200) yards [680 (760, 820, 960, 1020, 1090) meters] of aran weight yarn. Sample was knit in the colorway Manzanilla Olive and in size small.

NEEDLES

US 8 [5 mm] circular needles, 24″ [60 cm] long, and dpns. Adjust needle size if necessary to obtain the correct gauge.

NOTIONS

Three 1″ [2.5 cm] buttons (or bigger), tapestry needle, stitch markers, stitch holders/waste yarn and blocking aids.

Sizing

XS (S, M, L, XL, XXL)

Finished chest circumference: 30 (34, 38, 42, 46, 50)″ [75 (85, 95, 105, 115, 125) cm]. The jacket is intended to be worn with no ease.

Gauge

16 sts and 21 rows = 4″ [10 cm] in Stockinette stitch.

Finished measurements

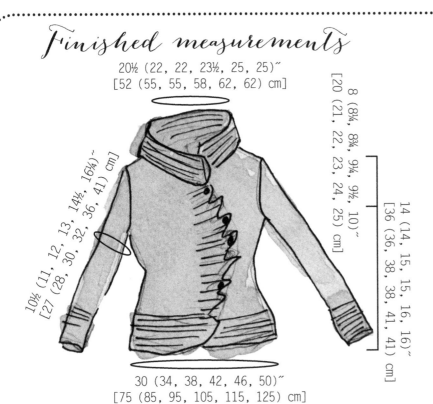

20½ (22, 22, 23½, 25, 25)″
[52 (55, 55, 58, 62, 62) cm]

8 (8¼, 8¾, 9¼, 9½, 10)″
[20 (21, 22, 23, 24, 25) cm]

14 (14, 15, 15, 16, 16)″
[36 (36, 38, 38, 41, 41) cm]

10¾ (11, 12, 13, 14½, 16¼)″
[27 (28, 30, 32, 36, 41) cm]

30 (34, 38, 42, 46, 50)″
[75 (85, 95, 105, 115, 125) cm]

Collar

Note: The collar is worked in garter st and shaped with short rows. The inside of the folded piece is the RS. Don't pick up the wraps, they will blend nicely in garter st..

Using circular needle CO 90 (96, 96, 102, 108, 108) sts. Do not join. Knit one row (WS).

BEGIN SHORT ROWS

ROWS 1 AND 2 (RS and WS): k until 2 sts remain, W&T.

ROWS 3 AND 4 (RS and WS): k until one st before previous wrapped st remains, W&T.

Repeat rows 3 and 4 two times more.

ROWS 5 AND 6 (RS and WS): k until 30 sts remain, W&T.

ROWS 7 AND 8 (RS and WS): k two stitches past the previous wrapped st (the stitch closer to the center, not the wrapped stitches from rows 3 and 4), W&T.

Repeat rows 7 and 8 two times more. Work again rows 3 and 4 (now working to the wrapped stitches closer to the end, past the wrapped sts from rows 7 and 8) four times more.

ROW 9 (RS): k until 64 (70, 70, 76, 82, 82) sts remain, pm, ssk, k until 26 sts remain, k2tog, pm, k

until you've knit the previous wrapped st, W&T. *Note: there will be two wraps around the same stitch.*

Row 10 (WS): k until you've knit the previous wrapped st, W&T.

Row 11 (RS): k to m, sm, ssk, k until two sts before m remain, k2tog, sm, k until you've knit the previous wrapped st, W&T.

Row 12 (WS): k until you've knit the previous wrapped st, W&T.

Repeat rows 11 and 12 two times more [*8 sts decreased; 82 (88, 88, 94, 100, 100) sts remain*]. Continue repeating only row 12 (RS and WS) until only 1 st after wrapped st remain. Knit to end on next WS row.

Yoke

*Note: The yoke is worked with simultaneous set-in sleeves in which the shoulder stitches are cast-on using backwards-loop cast-on method and the neck is shaped with short rows. At first, you will need both the circular needle **and** your double-pointed needles for it. After a few increase rows, you can easily work all stitches with the circular needle again.*

Work in St st and the button band in garter st. First you will cast-on stitches for shoulders and shape both the back and the front of the neck simultaneously as follows:

Row 13 (RS): Work 9 sts in garter st for button band, k15 (17, 17, 19, 21, 21), CO 9 (12, 14, 15, 17, 18) sts using backwards-loop cast-on method on one dpn (front of left shoulder stitches), pick up and knit 9 (12, 14, 15, 17, 18) sts from the cast-on edge using another dpn (back of left shoulder stitches), working

with circular needle k2, turn work.

Row 14 (WS): yo, p to dpn, p sts on dpn until 1 sts remain, slip the last st, pm, m1R (purl), change to next dpn and m1L (purl), pm, slip the next st, p to end of the second dpn, using circular needle p1, turn work.

Row 15 (RS; *work all sts using the same circular needle if possible, otherwise continue to work the shoulder sts with dpns*): yo, k to m, sm, m1L, k to m, m1R, sm, k to previous yo, k2tog the yo with the next st, turn work.

Row 16 (WS): yo, p until 1 st before m remain, slip the next st, sm, m1R (purl), p to m, m1L (purl), sm, p to previous yo, sssp the yo with the next two sts, turn work.

Work rows 15 and 16 two times more.

Row 17 (RS): yo, k to m, m1L, sm, k to m, m1R, sm, k to previous yo, k2tog the yo with the next st, k until 24 (26, 26, 28, 30, 30) sts remain, CO 9 (12, 14, 15, 17, 18) sts using backwards-loop cast-on method on one dpn (back of right shoulder stitches), pick up and knit 9 (12, 14, 15, 17, 18) sts from the cast-on edge using another dpn (front of right shoulder stitches), working with circular needle k1, turn work.

Row 18 (WS): yo, p to dpn, p sts on dpn until 1 sts remain, slip the last st on dpn, pm, m1R (purl), change to next dpn and m1L (purl), pm, slip the next st, p to end of the second dpn, using circ needle k2, turn work.

Row 19 (RS; *work all sts using the same circular needle if possible, otherwise continue to work the shoulder sts with dpns*): yo, k to m, sm, m1L, k to m, m1R, sm, k to previous yo, k3tog the yo with the next two sts, turn work.

Row 20 (WS): yo, p until 1 st before m remain, slip the next st, sm, m1R (purl), p to m, m1L (purl), sm, p to previous yo, ssp the yo with the next st, turn work.

Work rows 19 and 20 two times more.

Continue working short rows for front of the neck

Row 21 (RS): yo, k to m, sm, m1L, k to m, m1R, sm, k to previous yo, k3tog the yo with the next two sts, turn work.

Row 22 (WS): yo, p until 1 st before m remain, slip the next st, sm, m1R (purl), p to m, m1L (purl), sm, p to previous yo, ssp the yo with the next st, p until 1 st before m remain, slip the next st, sm, m1R (purl), p to m, m1L (purl), sm, p to previous yo, sssp the yo with the next two sts, turn work.

Row 23 (RS): yo, k to m, sm, m1L, k to m, m1R, sm, k to m (the back stitches), sm, m1L, k to m, m1R, sm, k to previous yo, k3tog the yo with the next two stitches, turn work.

Row 24 (WS): yo, p until 1 st before m remain, slip the next st, sm, m1R (purl), p to m, m1L (purl), sm, p until 1 st before m remain, slip the next st, sm, m1R (purl), p to m, m1L (purl), sm, p to previous yo, sssp the yo with the next two sts, turn work.

Work rows 23 and 24 — 1 (2, 2, 3, 4, 4) time(s) more. Work end of row as follows (RS and WS):

Row 25 (RS): yo, k to m, sm, m1L, k to m, m1R, sm, k to m (the back stitches), sm, m1L, k to m, m1R, sm, k to previous yo, k3tog the yo with the next two stitches, k to end.

Row 26 (WS): k9 (button band in garter stitch),

p until 1 st before m remain, slip the next st, sm, m1R (purl), p to m, m1L (purl), sm, p until 1 st before m remain, slip the next st, sm, m1R (purl), p to m, m1L (purl), sm, p to previous yo, sssp the yo with the next two sts, p until 9 sts remain, k to end.

You have now 9 stitches in garter stitch for each button band, 17 (21, 23, 25, 28, 29) sts in St st for each front, 52 (60, 64, 68, 74, 76) sts in St st for the back and 30 (34, 34, 38, 42, 42) sts between markers for each sleeve.

Continue with button band increases and button band short rows and working even the Stockinette parts of the upper body.

Row 27 (RS): k3, m1L, *k to m, sm; repeat three times from *, k until 3 sts remain, m1L, k to end.

Short row A (WS): k until 2 sts of the garter st button band remain, W&T.

Short row B (RS): k until 3 sts remain, m1L, k to end.

Short row C (WS): k until 1 st of the garter st button band remains, W&T.

Short row D (RS): k until 3 sts remain, m1L, k to end.

Row 28 (WS): k all button band stitches (garter st), *p until 1 st before m remain, slip the next st, sm, p to m, sm, slip the next st; repeat once from *, p to button band in garter st, k to end.

Repeat rows 27 to 28 (including the short rows of right front button band) until the armhole depth along the slipped stitch line measures 6 (6¼, 6¾, 6¾, 7, 7)″ [15 (16, 17, 17, 18, 18) cm].

Begin underarm increases

*Note: continue button band short rows A-D as established between each RS and WS row and front increases on both sides until you have **19 stitches** in garter st for the left front button band and **29 stitches** in garter st for the right button band. Omit front increases after that.*

Row 29 (RS): k3, m1L, *k until 4 sts before m remain, m1R, k to m, sm, k3, m1L, k until 3 sts before m remain, m1R, k to m, sm, k4, m1L; repeat once from *, k until 3 sts remain, m1L, k to end.

Row 30 (WS): k all button band stitches (garter st), *p until 1 st before m remain, slip the next st, sm, p to m, sm, slip the next st; repeat once from *, p to button band in garter st, k to end.

Work rows 29 and 30 — 3 (3, 3, 4, 5, 6) times more working the short rows A-D as established and placing first buttonhole on second time working row 29: work as established until you have worked 14 stitches of the right button band, k2tog, yo, work to end. Repeat the buttonhole two more times every 4″ [10 cm] measuring from the garter stitch button band laid flat.

Divide for body and sleeves

(RS): *work to m, remove marker, place the sts before next m on holder for sleeve, CO 0 (0, 0, 2, 2, 5) sts using backwards-loop cast-on method, pm, CO 0 (0, 0, 2, 2, 5) sts using backwards-loop cast-on method, remove m; repeat once from *, work to end.

You have now 38 (42, 42, 48, 52, 54) sts on each holder for sleeves and 152 (166, 174, 194, 210, 230) sts on the needle for the body.

Body

Continue even, working button bands in garter stitch and rest of body in Stockinette stitch. Work short rows A-D until all three buttonholes are worked. When body measures 3″ [8 cm] from underarm, begin waist shaping.

Decrease row (RS): *work as established until 5 sts before m remain, k2tog, k to m, sm, k 3, ssk; repeat once from *, work to end.

Repeat the decrease row three more times on every 4th row (16 sts decreased). Work even additional 2″ [5 cm], but begin decreases of right button band: work as established until 5 sts remain, k2tog, k to end. Work the button band decrease row every 6th row all the way to end of the body.

Increase row (RS): *work as established until 4 sts before m remain, m1R, k to m, k 4, m1L; repeat once from *, work to end.

Repeat the increase row three more times on every 4th row (16 sts increased). Continue as established until the body measures 11″ [28 cm] from underarm. Work additional 3″ [8 cm] in garter st. BO sts loosely.

Sleeves

Place the 38 (42, 42, 48, 52, 54) sts of sleeve from holder on dpns. Pick up 4 (2, 4, 4, 4, 10) from the underarm to achieve the intended upper arm width, **do not decrease these stitches**. *Note: You can pick up a few extra stitches from the underarm for all sizes to prevent hole – or sew the gap while finishing the garment. Decrease these extra picked up stitches on next possible round.*

Join yarn to the middle of the picked up stitches and pm to indicate beginning of the round. Work even in St st until the sleeve measures 4″ [10 cm] from underarm.

DECREASE ROUND: k2, ssk, k until 4 sts remain, k2tog, k to end.

Repeat the decrease round twice more every 2″ [5 cm]. Continue even in St st until the sleeve measure 11″ [28 cm] from underarm. Work additional 3″ [8 cm] in garter st (alternate k and p rounds). BO sts loosely.

Finishing

Weave in all yarn ends and sew on buttons to left front. Try on the jacket to determine the best placement of the buttons. Wet block the jacket to measurements.

Ground

The clean design of this open, loose-fitting vest makes it a wonderfully versatile piece that works anywhere from the office to a more informal setting. The vest is a fun and smooth knitting project, worked in one piece with garter stitch and shaped using short rows.

Materials

Yarn

4 (5, 5, 6, 7, 7) skeins of Tosh Sport by Madelinetosh (100% superwash merino wool; 270 yds [247 m] /skein). Approx. 1080 (1240, 1380, 1520, 1650, 1800) yards [990 (1140, 1260, 1390, 1530, 1670) meters] of heavy sport weight yarn. Sample was knit in the colorway Cousteau in size small.

Needles

US 8 [5 mm] circular needles, 24″ [60 cm] long. Adjust needle size if necessary to obtain the correct gauge.

Notions

Tapestry needle, stitch markers, stitch holders/waste yarn and blocking aids.

Sizing

XS (S, M, L, XL, XXL)

Finished width of the back: 16½ (19, 21, 23¼, 25½, 27¾)″ [42 (47, 53, 58, 63, 69) cm]. The vest is intended to be worn with a few inches of positive ease.

Gauge

18 sts and 30 rows = 4″ [10 cm] in garter stitch.

Finished measurements

12 (13¼, 14½, 15½, 16½, 18¾)˝
30 (33, 36, 39, 42, 47) cm

30˝
[75 cm]

16½ (19, 21, 23¼, 25½, 27¾)˝
[42 (47, 53, 58, 63, 69) cm]

Upper body

Using circular needle CO 200 (200, 210, 220, 230, 240) sts. Work back and forth in garter st until the piece measures 2˝ [5 cm].

On next row (RS) place markers for yoke increases: k 60 (60, 65, 70, 75, 80), pm, k 10, pm, k 20, pm, k 20, pm, k 20, pm, k 10, pm, k 60 (60, 65, 70, 75, 80) sts to end. Continue in garter st increasing for yoke and decreasing for the fronts on every second RS row –

INC/DEC ROW (RS): k1, ssk, k to marker, m1R, sm, k to m, m1R, sm, k to m, m1R, sm, k to m, sm, m1L, k to m, sm, m1L, k to m, sm, m1L, k until 3 sts remain, k2tog, k1.

Continue as established until you have worked 18 (21, 23, 25, 26, 30) increase/decrease rows. Work additional 1˝ [2.5 cm] in garter st and decrease for the fronts on every second RS row as established, ending on a WS row.

Lower body

On next row, BO the sleeve stitches and remove all markers (RS): k until 83 (93, 103, 113, 123, 138) sts before the third marker remain. BO the next 55 (60, 65, 70, 75, 85) sts (sleeve opening), k the next 76 (86, 96, 106, 116, 126) and BO the next 55 (60, 65, 70, 75, 85) sts, W&T (around the first stitch after the bound-off stitches of the sleeve).

SHORT ROWS FOR THE BACK

Note: in the short rows you will work only the 76 (86, 96, 106, 116, 126) sts of the back and decrease one stitch of the front on every row.

ROW 1 (WS): k 76 (86, 96, 106, 116, 126) sts of the back, W&T (work the wrap around the first stitch after the bound-off stitches of the sleeve opening).

ROW 2 (RS): k until one st before previous wrapped st remain, ssk, W&T.

ROW 3 (WS): k until one st before previous wrapped st remain, k2tog, W&T.

Repeat short rows 2 and 3 until all stitches of the fronts are used up. End with WS row. Cut yarn and leave back stitches on needle.

With RS facing, re-attach yarn the slanting left front edge. Pick up and knit stitches in ratio 1 st on every second row (one stitch form each purl ridge) from left front edge, knit the stitches of the back and pick up and knit stitches in ratio 1 st on every second row from right front edge.

Work back and forth in garter st until the vest measures 29½" [75 cm] from collar. BO sts loosely.

Finishing

Weave in all yarn ends. Wet block the vest to measurements.

Red and Pink

Red
like an apple's cheek
on Christmas Day

While blue and green are soothing and calm colors, red, pink
and their companion purple are
more likely to cause a stir -
for better or worse. Especially
it is traditionally described
as a dynamic color, attracting
attention. It is the color of
love and courage, but also of
impulsiveness and even danger.

RED is a primary color in many senses. In the development of languages, red is usually the first color name,
emerging in a language after the words for black and
white. It is also believed that red is one of the oldest
colors in the history of art: red from ochre or manga-
nese was used to paint caves and stone objects more
than 30,000 years ago.

For thousands of years, the most significant and
widely used red dye was produced from the roots of
the plant *madder*. One of the most desirable and valuable madder-based red dye was a bright and durable
dye called Turkey red, which had been known in Asia
and the Middle-East long before it reached Europe.
The production method was known as well in ancient
Egypt as in ancient India. The recipe was long kept
secret from Europeans, who did not discover it until
centuries later.

In year 1868, German chemists discovered synthetic red, *alizarin*, the coloring matter of madder. The
massive European madder fields were quickly abando-
ned and replaced by vineyards. Alizarin is still sometimes in use, but not as widely as it was earlier.

PINK, the whitish hue of color red, is today probably
the most gendered of all colors. It has a strong associa-
tion with stereotypical femininity, from prettiness and
tenderness to lack of authority. It is disputed when and
why pink turned into a girly color and became a widely accepted norm, since as late as early 20th century
many considered pink as a strong and decisive color
and thus more appropriate for boys than girls.

PURPLE has many associations that date back to
centuries: magic, mystery, spirituality, mourning,
creativity, intellectuality and royalty. What is perhaps
in common in all these associations is that purple is
something out of the ordinary. Purple is quite rare in
nature, which may have contributed to its unworldly
associations.

To ancient Greeks and Romans, purple was the
most sacred color of all. The Purple dye used in the
ancient times, known as Tyrian purple, was extracted
from a particular species of shellfish and the color was
reserved for the emperors and priests. Tyrian purple
had the unique advantage that it did not fade but became more intense with time.

Mauve, a particular shade of purple (or violet, depending on use of terms), was the first synthetic color
that was discovered. It marked the beginning of a color
revolution, and foundation for a whole new industry
of completely synthetic dyes was born.

Little Miss Frill

EVERY LITTLE MISS NEEDS A LOVELY LIGHTWEIGHT PULLOVER WITH LOTS OF ROOM TO PLAY. THE TIGHT HERRINGBONE PATTERN KEEPS THE DETAILS CLEAR AND MAKES THE PIECE BOTH FLATTERING AND FUN TO KNIT.

Materials

YARN

2 (2, 3, 3, 3, 3) skeins of Traveler Sport by The Plucky Knitter (65% merino, 20% silk, 15% yak; 325 yds [295 m] per skein). Approx. 550 (640, 720, 800, 880, 960) yards [500 (580, 660, 730, 800, 880) meters] of light sport weight yarn. Sample was knit in the colorway Hotsy Totsy in size 6.

NEEDLES

US 4 [3.5 mm] and US 8 [5 mm] circular needles, 24" [60 cm] long, and dpns. Adjust needle size if necessary to obtain the correct gauge.

NOTIONS

Tapestry needle, stitch markers, stitch holders/waste yarn and blocking aids.

Sizing

2 (4, 6, 8, 10, 12) YEARS

Finished chest circumference: 26 (28, 30, 32, 34, 36)" [65 (70, 75, 80, 85, 90) cm]. Choose a size with minimum of 4" [10 cm] of positive ease.

Gauge

22 sts and 28 rows = 4" [10 cm] in Stockinette stitch using smaller needle.

Finished measurements

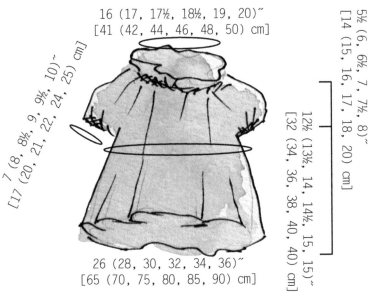

16 (17, 17½, 18½, 19, 20)˝
[41 (42, 44, 46, 48, 50) cm]

5½ (6, 6½, 7, 7½, 8)˝
[14 (15, 16, 17, 18, 20) cm]

7 (8, 8½, 9, 9½, 10)˝
[17 (20, 21, 22, 24, 25) cm]

12½ (13½, 14, 14½, 15, 15)˝
[32 (34, 36, 38, 40, 40) cm]

26 (28, 30, 32, 34, 36)˝
[65 (70, 75, 80, 85, 90) cm]

Stitch patterns

HERRINGBONE PATTERN (IN THE ROUND)

ROUND 1: k2tog slipping the first st off the needle, *k2tog the remaining st with the next st, slip only the first st off the needle; repeat from * to end of rnd.

ROUND 2: k2tog tbl slipping the first st off the left needle, *k2tog tbl the remaining st with the next st, slip only the first st off the needle; repeat from * to end of rnd.

Note: When you come to beg of rnd marker (one st remaining), remove m and work the last and first st as on previous rnd (k2tog or k2tog tbl), slip first st off the needle and pm for beg of rnd.

3×1-RIBBING

*K3, p1; repeat from * to end of round.

Collar

Using smaller circular needle, CO 180 (184, 192, 204, 212, 220) sts. Join in round carefully not twisting your stitches and pm for beginning of round. Work in St st for 3″ [8 cm]. Decrease on next round: work k2tog to end of round [*90 (92, 96, 102, 106, 110) sts remain*]. Change to larger needle and work in herringbone pattern for 8 rounds.

[54]............ red and pink

Yoke

Change to smaller needle and continue with increase round: *k1, m1R; repeat from * to end of round [*180 (184, 192, 204, 212, 220) sts*].

Raglan increases

Round 1 (setup round): k 34 (36, 38, 40, 42, 44), pm, k 56 (56, 58, 62, 64, 66), pm, k 34 (36, 38, 40, 42, 44), pm, k 56 (56, 58, 62, 64, 66) to end.

Round 2: *k2, m1L, sm, k until 2 sts before m remain, m1R, k2; repeat three times from *.

Round 3: k to end slipping markers.

Work rounds 2 and 3 — 7 (9, 11, 12, 14, 16) times more. After all increase rounds you have *244 (264, 288, 308, 332, 356) sts* on needle.

Divide for body and sleeves

*Remove m, place stitches before next marker on holder/waste yarn for sleeve, sm, k to m; repeat once from *.

You have now 50 (56, 62, 66, 72, 78) sts on each holder

for sleeves and 144 (152, 164, 176, 188, 200) sts on the needle for the body.

Body

Continue even working St st. When the body measures 2″ [5 cm] from underarm, begin increases —

INCREASE ROUND (RS): *sm, k3, m1L, k until 3sts before m remain, m1R, k2; repeat once from *.

Repeat the increase round on every 6th round. Continue even in St st until body measures 11 (12, 13, 13½, 14, 14)″ [28 (30, 32, 34, 36, 36) cm]. Work 1½″ [4 cm] in 3×1 rib (k3, p1). BO sts loosely in 3×1 ribbing.

Sleeves

Note: You can pick a few extra stitches from the underarm for all sizes to prevent hole – or sew the gap while finishing the garment. Decrease these extra picked up stitches on next possible round.

Place the 50 (56, 62, 66, 72, 78) sts of sleeve from holder on smaller dpns. Pm to indicate beginning of the round and join yarn. Work even in St st until the sleeve measures 1 (1, 2, 2, 2, 2)″ [2.5 (2.5, 5, 5, 5, 5) cm] from underarm.

DECREASE ON NEXT ROUND: *k2tog, k2 (2, 1, 1, 1, 1); repeat from * 11 (11, 15, 15, 19, 21) times more, k to end of round [*38 (44, 46, 50, 52, 56) sts remain*].

Change to larger needle and work in herringbone pattern for 8 rounds. Change to smaller needle and increase on next rnd: k 2 (2, 1, 1, 1, 1), m1R; repeat from * 11 (11, 15, 15, 19, 21) times more, k to end of round. Work even in St st for additional 3″ [8 cm]. BO sts loosely.

Finishing

Weave in all yarn ends. Block the pullover to measurements using your preferred method.

RED

red and pink [57]

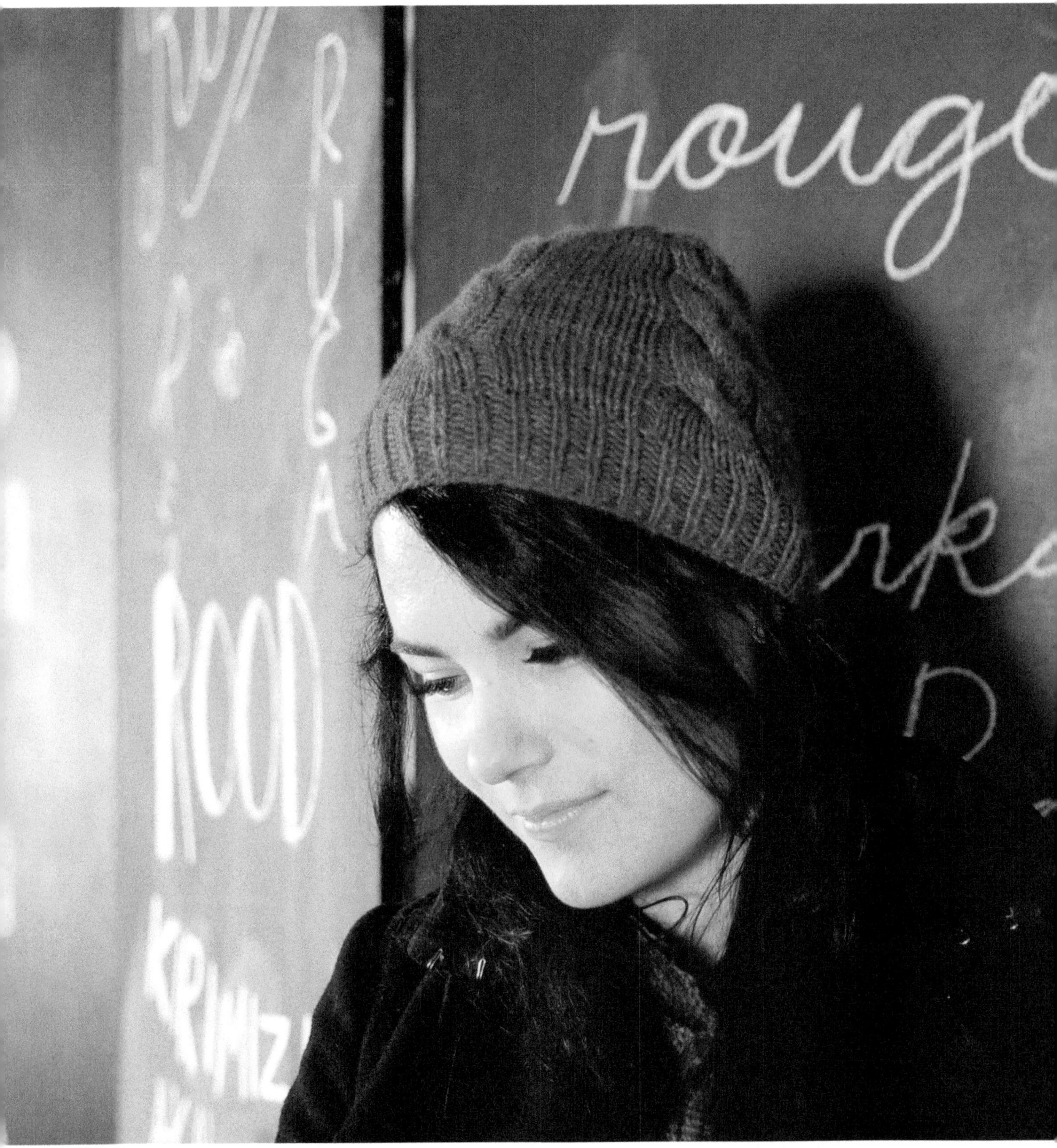
rouge
ROOD

Classic Cables

THIS WARM AND SWEET BEANIE WITH CLASSIC CABLES IS A FUN AND QUICK KNIT. WHEN WORKED IN A MERINO BLEND LIKE PRIMO WORSTED, THE CABLES REALLY POP OUT.

Materials

YARN

1 skein of Primo Worsted by The Plucky Knitter (75% Merino, 20% Cashmere, 5% Nylon; 200 yards [183 meters] /100 grams). Approx. 180 yards [165 meters] of worsted weight yarn. Sample was knit in the colorway Love Notes.

NEEDLES

US 8 [5 mm] and US 4 [3.5 mm] circular needles, 16˝ [40 cm] long; US 8 [5 mm] dpn's. Adjust needle size if necessary to obtain the correct gauge.

NOTIONS

Cable needle, tapestry needle, stitch markers.

Sizing

ONE SIZE.

To fit head circumference 20-22˝ [51-56 cm]; finished brim circumference 18˝ [46 cm].

Gauge

16 sts and 26 rows = 4˝ [10 cm] in Stockinette stitch using larger needles.

Chart A

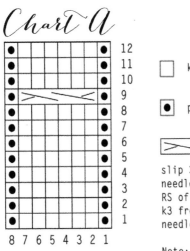

☐	knit
⊙	purl

slip 3 sts on cable needle and hold on RS of the work, k3, k3 from cable needle.

Note: Read the chart from right to left.

Stitch pattern

1×1 RIBBING

*k1, p1; repeat from * to end of round.

Brim

Using smaller circular needle and MC, CO 80 sts. Carefully join in round without twisting your stitches and pm for beginning of round. Work in 1×1 ribbing for 2″ [5 cm].

Body

Using MC, change to larger needle and continue in St st stitch and cables. Place cables on first round as follows: sm, *k8, work one repeat of row 1 in Chart A; repeat from * 4 times more. Continue in St st and cables, working through all rows of Chart A. Continue as established until the beanie measures 9″ [23 cm].

DECREASES

DECREASE ROUND 1: sm, *k2tog, k until 2 sts of the St st part remain, ssk, work the next row of Chart A; repeat 4 times more from *.

Repeat the decrease round 1 two more times (two sts remain on each St st part).

DECREASE ROUND 2: sm, *k2tog, work the next row of Chart A; repeat 4 times more from *.

DECREASE ROUND 3: sm, *k1, p1, k2tog, work the sts of cable in St st until 2 sts of cable remain, ssk, p1; repeat 4 times more from *.

Repeat decrease round 3 once (two sts remain on each cable part).

DECREASE ROUND 4: sm, *k1, p1, k2tog, p1; repeat 4 times more from *.

Break yarn leaving a long tail and thread through remaining stitches. Draw the tail tight and fasten off securely.

Finishing

Weave in all yarn ends. Block the beanie using your preferred method.

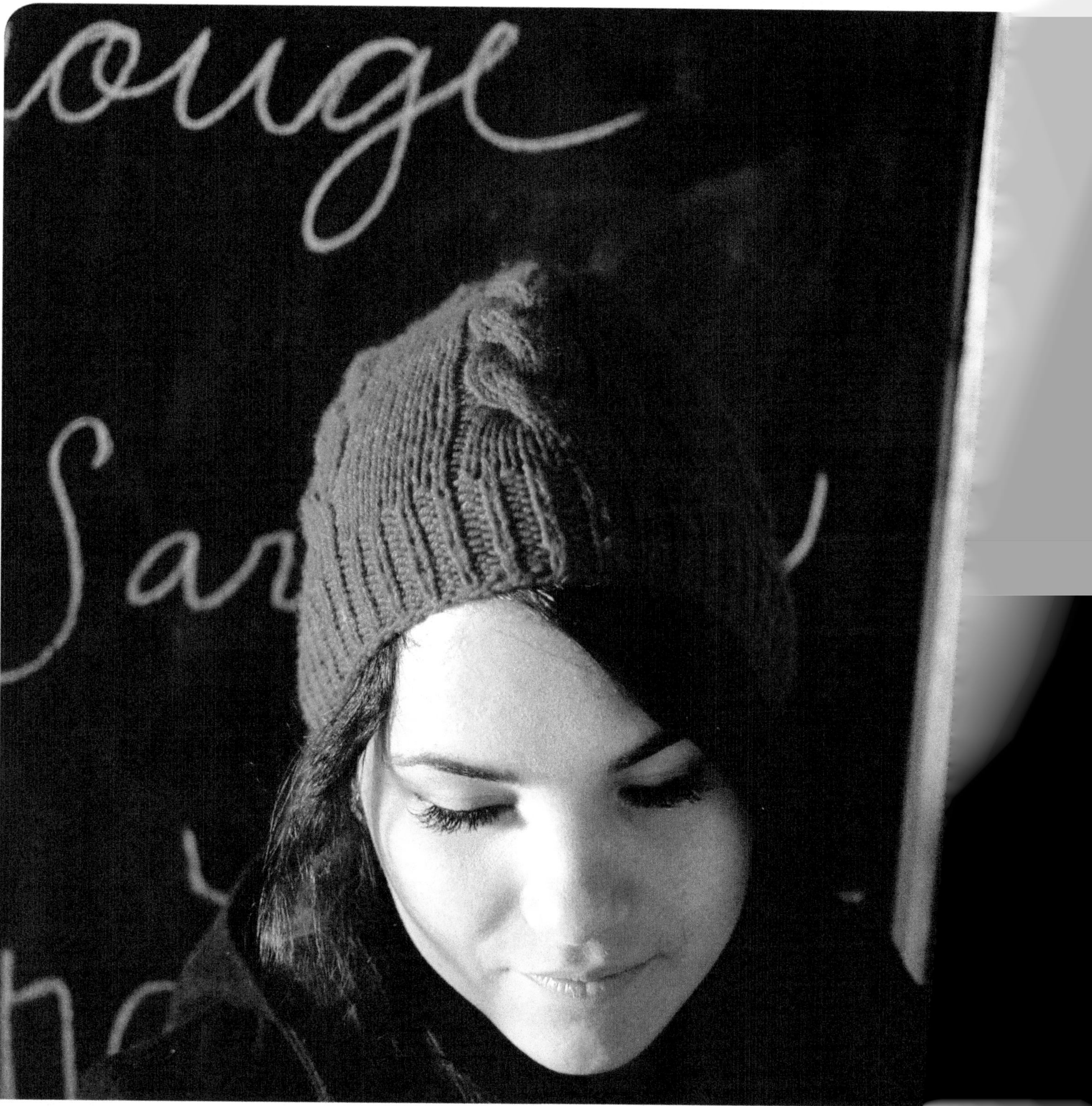

Little Red

LITTLE RED IS A LOVELY EVERYDAY CARDIGAN WITH PLENTY OF SOOTHING GARTER STITCH. IN THIS LIGHT PINK OR ROSY COLORWAY IT LOOKS BOTH SWEET AND COMFORTABLE.

Materials

YARN

4 (5, 5, 6, 6, 7) skeins of Tosh DK by Madelinetosh (100% merino, 225 yds [206 m] per skein). Approx. 900 (1000, 1100, 1200, 1280, 1380) yards [730 (800, 900, 1000, 1100, 1170) meters] of DK to worsted weight yarn. Sample was knit in the colorway Isadora and in size small.

NEEDLES

US 8 [5 mm] and US 6 [4 mm] circular needles, 24˝ [60 cm] long, and dpns. Adjust needle size if necessary to obtain the correct gauge.

NOTIONS

10 (10, 10, 11, 11, 12) 1˝ [2.5 cm] buttons, tapestry needle, stitch markers, stitch holders/waste yarn and blocking aids.

Sizing

XS (S, M, L, XL, XXL)

Finished chest circumference: 30 (34, 38, 42, 46, 50)˝ [75 (85, 95, 105, 115, 125) cm]. The cardigan is intended to be worn with no ease.

Gauge

18 sts and 30 rows = 4˝ [10 cm] in garter stitch using larger needles.

Finished measurements

21¼ (21, 21¼, 21¾, 23, 23½)″
[53 (52, 53, 55, 58, 59) cm]

7 (7½, 8, 9, 9½, 10)″
[18 (19, 20, 21, 23, 25) cm]

10½ (11, 12, 13, 14, 16)″
[27 (28, 30, 32, 36, 40) cm]

17½″
[42 cm]

30 (34, 38, 42, 46, 50)″
[75 (85, 95, 105, 115, 125) cm]

Yoke

Using larger circular needle, CO 90 (88, 90, 92, 98, 100) sts. Work in garter st and begin raglan increases as follows —

Row 1 (RS, setup row): k 12 (14, 15, 17, 18, 19), m1R, k2, pm, k2, m1L, k 10 (6, 4, 2, 2, 2), m1R, k2, pm, k2, m1L, k 30 (32, 36, 38, 42, 42), m1R, k2, pm, k2, m1L, k 10 (6, 4, 2, 2, 2), m1R, k2, pm, k2, m1L, k to end.

Row 2 (WS): k to end, slipping markers.

Row 3 (RS): *k until 2 sts before m remain, m1R, k2, pm, k2, m1L; repeat three times from *, k to end.

Row 4 (WS): k to end slipping markers.

Work rows 3 and 4 – 15 (18, 21, 24, 27, 31) times more. After all increase rounds you have *226 (248, 274, 300, 330, 364)* sts on needle.

DIVIDE FOR BODY AND SLEEVES

*K to m, remove m, place stitches before next marker on holder/waste yarn for sleeve, sm; repeat once from *, k to end.

You have now 48 (50, 54, 58, 64, 72) sts on each holder for sleeves and 130 (148, 166, 184, 202, 220) sts on the needle for the body.

Body

Continue even working garter stitch. When the body measures 3″ [8 cm] from underarm, begin waist shaping.

DECREASE ROW (RS): *k until 8 sts before m remain, k2tog, k to m, sm, k6, ssk; repeat once from *, k to end.

Repeat the decrease row three more times on every 6th row (*16 sts decreased; 114 (140, 150, 168, 186, 204) sts remain*). Work in garter st additional 2″ [5 cm].

INCREASE ROW (RS): *k until 7 sts before m remain, m1L, k to m, sm, k7, m1R; repeat once from *, k to end.

Repeat the increase row 4 more times on every 6th row (*16 sts increased; 130 (156, 166, 184, 202, 220) sts on needle*). Continue even in garter st until the body measures 15″ [38 cm] from underarm. Change to smaller circular needle and work 1½″ [4 cm] in 2×2 rib. BO sts loosely in ribbing.

Sleeves

Note: You can pick a few extra stitches from the underarm for all sizes to prevent hole – or sew the gap while finishing the garment. Decrease these extra picked up stitches on next possible round.

Place the 48 (50, 54, 58, 64, 72) sts of sleeve from holder on larger dpns. Pm to indicate beginning of the round and join yarn. Work even in garter st until the sleeve measures 4″ [10 cm] from underarm.

DECREASE ROUND (knit round): k2, ssk, k until 4 sts remain, k2tog, k to end.

Repeat the decrease round 2 (2, 2, 3, 3, 3) times more every 2″ [5 cm]. Work even garter st until sleeve measures 17½″ [44 cm]. Change to smaller dpns and work 1½″ [4 cm] in 2×2 rib. BO sts loosely in ribbing.

Hood

Using larger needle, pick up and knit 90 (88, 90, 92, 98, 100) sts from CO edge of yoke. Pm for the middle on first row: k 45 (44, 45, 46, 49, 50) sts pm, k to end. Work back and forth in garter st until the hood measures 1″ [2.5 cm] from neck edge. Place first and last 5 sts on separate holders. Start hood increases as follows —

INCREASE ROW (RS): k until 20 (19, 20, 21, 24, 25) sts before m remain, m1R, k to m, sm, k 20 (19, 20, 21, 24, 25), m1L, k to end.

Repeat the increase row 9 times more on every 4th row (20 sts increased; 100 (98, 100, 102, 108, 110) sts on needle). Work even in garter st until the hood measures 10″ [25 cm] from neck edge. Work short rows to shape the hood —

SETUP SHORT ROWS (RS and WS): k 5 sts past marker, W&T.

SHORT ROWS 1 AND 2 (RS and WS): k 2 sts past previous wrapped st, W&T.

Repeat the short rows 1 and 2 (RS and WS) until you have less than 10 sts after the wrapped sts. Knit to end on next RS row. Knit four rows. Place first half of stitches on dpn (all sts before marker) and fold the hood RS facing inside. BO all stitches using three-needle bind-off method (seam will be formed on WS).

Button placket

Note: The button band is worked all in one piece, starting from right front hem and continuing to the hood edge and finally left front edge. The given stitch counts may vary depending on your row gauge, pick up stitches approx. in ratio one stitch every two rows – one stitch from each purl ridge.

Using smaller circular needle, pick up and knit 82 (84, 86, 88, 92, 96) sts along the left front edge, pm, pick up and knit 1 st before hood, pm, knit the 5 sts from holder, pick up and knit 55 sts from hood edge up to hood top seam, pick up and knit 55 sts from hood edge down to held sts, knit the 5 sts from holder, pm, pick up and knit 1 st before left front edge, pm, pick up and knit 82 (84, 86, 88, 92, 96) sts along the left front edge.

CONTINUE IN RIBBING AS FOLLOWS —

WS ROW: Work to m in 2×2 ribbing, sm, p1, sm, work to m in 2×2 ribbing, sm, p1, sm, work to end in 2×2 ribbing.

RS ROW: Work to m in 2×2 ribbing, m1R (k or p – make sure the front ribbing stays continu-ous), k1, m1L (k or p — make sure the hood ribbing stays continuous), work to m in 2×2 rib-bing, m1R (k or p — make sure the hood ribbing stays continuous), k1, m1L (k or p — make sure the front ribbing stays continuous), work to end in 2×2 ribbing.

When ribbing measures ¾″ [2 cm] work button-holes to right front —*Note: if your stitch count varies from given, place the buttonholes evenly according to your own numbers.*

BUTTONHOLE ROW (RS): *work 6 sts in 2×2 ribbing, yo, p2tog; repeat 9 (9, 9, 10, 10, 11) times from *, work to end as established.

Continue in 2×2 ribbing until the ribbing measures 1½″ [4 cm] as established. BO all sts loosely in ribbing.

Finishing

Weave in all yarn ends and sew buttons to left front. Block the cardigan to measurements using your pre-ferred method.

Wonder Stripes

This pullover is a wonderful wardrobe essential with a modern twist — the stripe detail makes this truly a one-of-kind project. Wonder Stripes is worked from top down in one piece, and the sleeve caps and collar ribbings are shaped with short rows.

Materials

YARN

5 (5, 6, 6, 7) skeins of Primo Sport by The Plucky Knitter (75% merino, 20% cashmere, 5% nylon; 275 yds [251 m] per skein). Approx. 920 (1050, 1180, 1300, 1480) yards [840 (960, 1080, 1190, 1350) meters] of MC and 110 (120, 140, 160, 180) yards [100 (110, 130, 150, 170) meters] of CC. Sample was knit in the colorways Vanity (MC) and Lonesome Highway (CC); in size medium.

NEEDLES

US 6 [4 mm] and US 2½ [3 mm] circular needles, 32″ [80 cm] long, and dpns. Adjust needle size if necessary to obtain the correct gauge.

NOTIONS

Six 1″ [2.5 cm] buttons, tapestry needle, stitch markers, stitch holders/waste yarn and blocking aids.

Sizing

S (M, L, XL, XXL)

Finished chest circumference: 36 (40, 44, 48, 52)″ [90 (100, 110, 120, 130) cm]. Choose a size with a small amount of positive ease.

Gauge

20 sts and 32 rows = 4″ [10 cm] in Stockinette stitch using larger needle.

Finished measurements

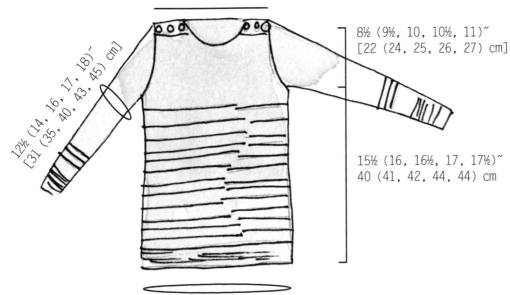

15½ (16½, 18, 20½, 22)″
[40 (42, 46, 52, 56) cm]

8½ (9½, 10, 10½, 11)″
[22 (24, 25, 26, 27) cm]

12½ (14, 16, 17, 18)″
[31 (35, 40, 43, 45) cm]

15½ (16, 16½, 17, 17½)″
40 (41, 42, 44, 44) cm

36 (40, 44, 48, 52)″
[90 (100, 110, 120, 130) cm]

Stitch pattern

TWISTED RIBBING

IN THE ROUND: *k1 tbl, p1; repeat from * to end of rnd.

BACK AND FORTH: *k1 tbl, p1; repeat from * to end on RS and *k1, p1 tbl; repeat from * to end on WS.

Upper body

The body is begun with shoulders and joined in the round after the garter stitch part.

LEFT FRONT —

Using larger circular needle and MC, CO 24 (26, 30, 34, 36) sts. Work back and forth in garter st 1″ [2.5 cm]. Work buttonholes on next row (RS): k 3 (4, 6, 6, 6), *ssk, yo, k6 (6, 6, 8, 9); repeat from * once, ssk, yo, k to end. Continue in garter st until the piece measures 3 (3, 4, 5, 5)″ [8 (8, 10, 12, 12 cm].

INCREASE ON NEXT ROW (RS): k3, m1L, k to end. Repeat the increase row every RS row 5 more times. End with WS row. Cut yarn and place sts on holder.

Right front —

Using larger circular needle and MC, CO 24 (26, 30, 34, 36) sts. Work back and forth in garter st 1″ [2.5 cm]. Work buttonholes on next row (RS): k 3 (4, 6, 6, 6), *ssk, yo, k6 (6, 6, 8, 9); repeat from * once, ssk, yo, k to end. Continue in garter st until the piece measures 4″ [8 (8, 10, 12, 12 cm].

Increase on next row (RS): knit until 3 sts remain, m1R, k to end. Repeat the increase row every RS row 5 more times. End with a WS row.

Join front pieces (RS)

Knit right front sts, CO 20 (20, 20, 24, 24) sts using backward-loop CO, knit left front sts from the holder (*you have 80 (84, 92, 104, 108) sts on needle*). Continue in garter st 1¼ (1¼, 1¾, 2¼, 2)″ [3 (3, 4, 6, 5) cm]. End with a RS row. Place front sts on holder.

Right back —

Using larger circular needle and MC, CO 24 (26, 30, 34, 36) sts. Work back and forth in garter st 3″ [8 cm].

Increase on next row (RS): k3, m1L, k to end. Repeat the increase row every RS row 5 more times. End with a WS row. Cut yarn and place sts on holder.

Left back —

Using larger circular needle and MC, CO 24 (26, 30, 34, 36) sts. Work back and forth in garter st 3″ [8 cm].

Increase on next row (RS): k until 3 sts remain, m1R, k to end. Repeat the increase row every RS row 5 more times. End with a WS row.

Join back pieces (RS)

Knit left back sts, CO 20 (20, 20, 24, 24) sts using backward-loop cast-on method, knit left front sts from holder (you have 80 (84, 92, 104, 108) sts on needle). Continue in garter st until the back piece is as long as the front piece. End with RS row.

Join front and back

The piece will be worked in one-piece and in the round, but the sleeve caps are shaped with short rows.

With WS of front and back facing each other, place the front sts on same circ needle – *note: you will pick up sts up the back edge for the sleeve next. Pick up sts through both layers, back and front, from the button plackets.* Pin down the shoulder button plackets so that you will have the buttonholes on top and in the highest point of shoulder.

Pick up and knit 26 (26, 29, 33, 31) sts up the back edge to buttonholes, pick up and knit 26 (26, 29, 33, 31) sts down the front edge to front stitches, pm, knit the 80 (84, 92, 104, 108) sts of front, pm, pick up and knit 26 (26, 29, 33, 31) sts up the front edge to buttonholes, pick up and knit 26 (26, 29, 33, 31) sts down the back edge to back stitches, pm, knit the 80 (84, 92, 104, 108) sts of back, pm (place a different colored marker for beginning of round).

Continue in St st and shape the sleeve caps with short rows

Setup row (RS): k 8 sts past top of shoulder (buttonholes), turn work.

Setup row (WS): yo, p 16, turn work.

SHORT ROW 1 (RS): yo, k to previous yo, k2tog the yo with the next st, turn work.

SHORT ROW 2 (WS): yo, p to previous yo, ssp the yo with the next st, turn work.

Repeat short rows 1 and 2 until you come to marker after k2tog. Continue to left sleeve cap: sm, k to m.

SETUP ROW (RS): k 8 sts past top of shoulder (buttonholes), turn work.

SETUP ROW (WS): yo, p 16, turn work.

SHORT ROW 1 (RS): yo, k to previous yo, k2tog the yo with the next st, turn work.

SHORT ROW 2 (WS): yo, p to previous yo, ssp the yo with the next st, turn work.

Repeat short rows 1 and 2 until you come to marker after k2tog. Work to end: sm, k to m. Work 1″ [2.5 cm] in St st. Start underarm increases: *k2, m1L, k until 2 sts before next m remain, m1R, k2, sm; repeat three more times from *. Repeat the increase round every second round 4 (5, 6, 5, 7) times more.

DIVIDE FOR BODY AND SLEEVES

Sm, place stitches before next marker on holder/waste yarn for sleeve, CO 0 (4, 4, 4, 6) sts using backward-loop CO, remove m, k to m, remove m, place stitches before next marker on holder/waste yarn for sleeve, CO 0 (4, 4, 4, 6) sts using backward-loop CO, remove m, k to end.

You have now 62 (64, 72, 78, 78) sts on each holder for sleeves and 180 (200, 220, 240, 260) sts on the needle for the body.

Lower body

Continue even working St st. When the body measures 1″ [2.5 cm] from underarm, begin striping: k 50 (60, 60, 70, 80), pm, work row 1 of chart A, pm, k to end with the same color you worked the last st of chart A.

Chart A

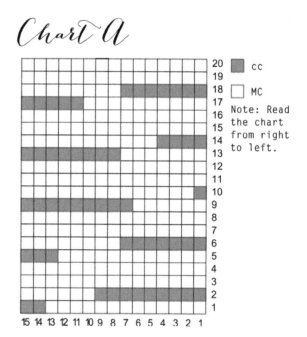

Work through chart A as established three times and work row 1 of chart A once more. Continue even in St st until body measures 14 (14¼, 14¾, 15, 15½)″ [36 (37, 38, 39, 40) cm]. Change to smaller circular needle and work 1½″ [4 cm] in twisted ribbing. BO sts loosely in ribbing.

Sleeves

Note: You can pick a few extra stitches from the underarm for all sizes to prevent hole – or sew the gap while finishing the garment. Decrease these extra picked up stitches on next possible round.

Place the 62 (64, 72, 78, 78) sts of sleeve from holder on smaller dpns. Pm to indicate beginning of the round and join yarn to underarm/middle of cast-on stitches. Pick up and knit 0 (2, 2, 2, 3) sts from the cast-on edge, knit to underarm and pick up and knit 0 (2, 2, 2, 3) sts from the cast-on edge to m. Work even in St st until the sleeve measures 2″ [5 cm] from underarm.

DECREASE ROUND: k2, ssk, k until 4 sts remain, k2tog, k to end.

Repeat the decrease round 2 (2, 2, 3, 3, 3) times more every 2″ [5 cm]. Work even in St st until sleeve measures 19″ [48 cm]. Change to smaller dpns needle and work 1½″ [4 cm] in twisted ribbing. BO sts loosely in ribbing.

Collar

FRONT

Using smaller circ needle and MC, pick up and knit 30 sts down the vertical edge of collar (*or one st every two rows if your row gauge differs significantly*), pick up and knit 20 (20, 20, 24, 24) sts from CO edge, pick up and knit 30 sts up the second vertical edge of collar.

Work in twisted ribbing and on next RS row begin short row shaping:

SETUP ROW (RS): work in ribbing until all sts from horizontal edge are worked in twisted rib, turn work.

SETUP ROW (WS): yo, work in twisted rib to end of horizontal edge, turn work.

SHORT ROW 3 (RS): yo, work in twisted rib to previous yo, k2tog tbl/p2tog the yo with the next st (depending on next st), turn work.

SHORT ROW 4 (WS): yo, work in twisted rib to previous yo, ssp/ssk the yo with the next st, turn work.

Repeat short rows 3 and 4 nine more times. Continue in twisted ribbing until the ribbing measures 1½″ [4 cm] in the deepest part. Work 4 rows in St st and BO sts loosely.

BACK

Work the back piece similarly, but pick up only 20 sts along the vertical edges (*or one st every two rows if your row gauge differs significantly*).

Finishing

Weave in all yarn ends. Sew on buttons to both shoulders. Block the pullover to measurements using your preferred method.

Afloat in Red

TUNE INTO DEEP RED WITH THIS WONDERFULLY SHAPED OPEN CARDIGAN. THE CARDIGAN IS VERSATILE AND WARM; IT HAS THE LONG LINE OF A BOYFRIEND-STYLE CARDIGAN, BUT WITH A MORE FITTED SHAPE. IT'S SHAPED WITH PLENTY OF SHORT ROWS AND HAS GREAT BIG POCKETS.

Materials

YARN

4 (5, 5, 6, 6, 6) skeins of Merino Sport by The Uncommon Thread (100% superwash merino; 286 yds [262 m] per skein). Approx. 1100 (1200, 1280, 1380, 1470, 1560) yards [1000 (1100, 1170, 1260, 1350, 1430) meters] of sport weight yarn. Sample was knit in the colorway Lust and in size small.

NEEDLES

US 7 [4.5 mm] and US 4 [3.5 mm] circular needles, 32″ [80 cm] long, and dpns. Adjust needle size if necessary to obtain the correct gauge.

NOTIONS

Tapestry needle, stitch markers, stitch holders/waste yarn and blocking aids.

Sizing

XS (S, M, L, XL, XXL)

Finished chest circumference: 30 (34, 38, 42, 46, 50)″ [75 (85, 95, 105, 115, 125) cm]. Choose a size with no ease or a small amount of positive ease.

Gauge

20 sts and 30 rows = 4″ [10 cm] in Stockinette stitch using smaller needle.

Finished measurements

13 (13, 13, 13¾, 14, 14)˝
[30 (30, 30, 34, 35, 35) cm]

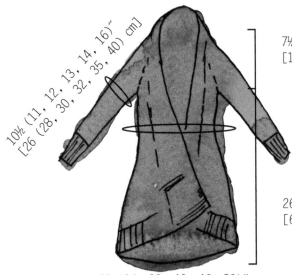

10½ (11, 12, 13, 14, 16)˝
[26 (28, 30, 32, 35, 40) cm]

7½ (8, 8½, 9, 9½, 10)˝
[19 (20, 21, 22, 24, 25) cm]

26 (26, 26, 26½, 27, 27)˝
[66 (66, 66, 67, 68, 68) cm]

30 (34, 38, 42, 46, 50)˝
[75 (85, 95, 105, 115, 125) cm]

Collar & front bands

Using smaller circular needle, CO 240 (248, 256 272, 284, 296) sts. Do not join. Work back and forth in 1×1 rib until piece measures 1˝ [2.5 cm]. Change to larger needle and continue in St st but work the first and last 10 sts in rib for bottom edge. Pm for the center (RS): work 10 sts in rib, k 110 (114, 118, 126, 132, 138) pm, work to end. Increase for hem every 1½˝ [3 cm] as follows (measuring from bottom ribbing):

INC ROW (RS): work 10 sts in rib, m1L, k until 10 sts remain, m1R, work to end in rib.

START SHORT ROW SHAPING FOR FRONT BANDS —

Note: work hem increases as established every 1½˝ [3 cm].

SHORT ROW SET 1 (left front band): work 10 sts in rib, k34, turn work; *yo, p to ribbing, work to end in rib, turn work; work 10 sts in rib, k to previous yo, k2tog the yo with the next st, k8, turn work; repeat 5 more times from *; yo, p to ribbing, work to end in rib.

WHOLE ROW (RS): work 10 sts in rib, k to the last yo, k2tog the yo with the next st, k until 10 sts remain, work to end in rib.

SHORT ROW SET 2 (right front band): work 10 sts in rib, p34, turn work; *yo, k to ribbing, work to end in rib, turn work; work 10 sts in rib, p to previous yo, ssp the yo with the next st, p8, turn work; repeat 5 more times from *; yo, k to ribbing, work to end in rib.

Work 1″ [2.5 cm] even in St st and 10 edge sts in rib and on first row ssp the last yo with the next st.

Add pockets

On RS row, place the first 42 sts on larger dpn. Working with two dpns, work back and forth as follows: work 10 sts in rib, work in St st until 10 sts remain, work to end in rib. Continue to work hem increases as established every 1½″ [3 cm], for left pocket work a m1L increase after the hem ribbing. Continue until the piece measures at bottom edge 12″ [30 cm]. Place pocket sts on holder and cut yarn. Place the last 42 sts on larger dpn, join yarn and work the right pocket similarly, now working a m1R increase before hem ribbing.

Continue with middle piece

First add pocket lining stitches to both ends of the front bands and collar as follows: CO 30 sts on larger dpn and work 1″ [2.5 cm] back and forth in St st with two dpns. Leave sts on dpn and cut yarn. CO 30 sts to larger circ needle and work in St st for 1″ [2.5 cm]. Join lining pieces to middle stitches (RS): work 30 sts on circ needle, k to end in St st and work 30 sts from dpn. Work the next WS row in St st.

Work short row shaping as follows:

Short row set 3 (left front band): k34, turn work; *yo, p to end, turn work; k to previous yo, k2tog the yo with the next st, k8, turn work; repeat 5 more times from *; yo, p to end.

Whole row (RS): k to end.

Short row set 4 (right front band): p34, turn work; *yo, k to end, turn work; p to previous yo, ssp the yo with the next st, p8, turn work; repeat 5 more times from *, yo, k to end.

Work 1″ [2.5 cm] even in St st. Alternate short row ses 3 and 4 and 1″ [2.5 cm] of St st until the middle piece reaches the pocket stitches on holder, ending with a WS row. Cut yarn.

Join pocket stitches to middle stitches

(RS): Place left pocket sts on larger dpn and join yarn. Work 10 sts in ribbing, work in St st until 30 sts remain, hold dpn at front of circ needle and *k2tog using one st from each needle; repeat from * until all sts from dpn are used up. K until 30 sts remain on circ needle, place the right pocket sts on dpn and hold at front of circ needle. *k2tog *k2tog using one st from each needle; repeat from * until all sts from circ needle are used up, work to end with the stitches on dpn.

Work the next row (WS) to end in St st but work the first and last 10 sts in rib for bottom edge.

Yoke

Change to smaller needle and continue with yoke increases and short rows —

Row 1 (setup row, RS): Work as established until 34 (34, 34, 35, 36, 36) sts before m remain, m1R, k1, pm, k1, m1L, k 12 (10, 8, 7, 6, 6), m1R, k1, pm, k1, m1L, k 36 (40, 44, 48, 52, 52) and at the same time remove the middle marker, m1R, k1, pm, k1, m1L, k 12 (10, 8, 7, 6, 6), m1R, k1, pm, k1, m1L, k1, turn work.

Row 2 (WS): yo, p to last marker, sm, p3, turn work.

Row 3 (RS): yo, *k until 1 st before m remain,

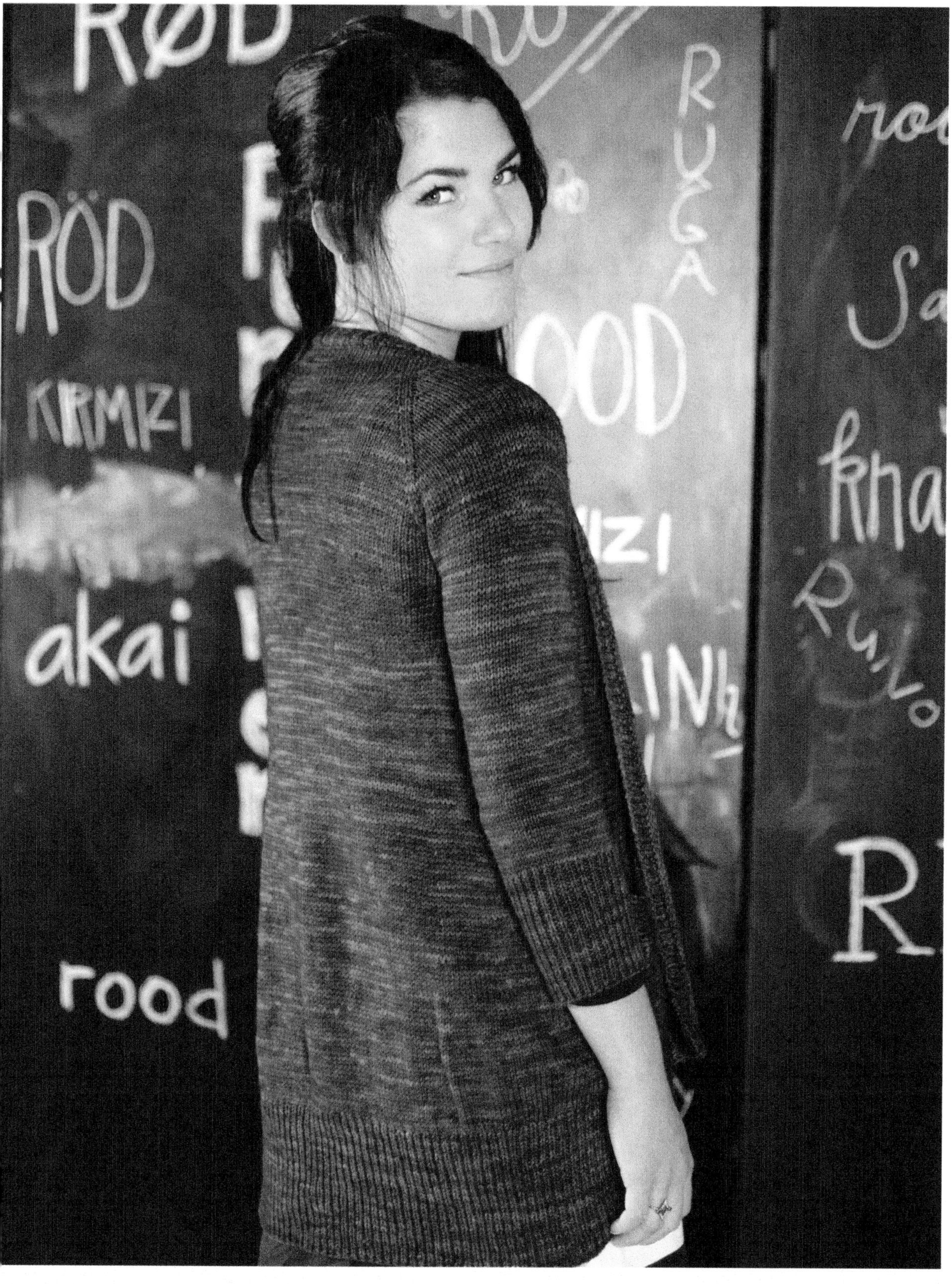
RØD
RÖD
KIRMIZI
akai
rood

m1R, k1, sm, k1, m1L; repeat three times from *, k until 1 st before previous yo remains, sssk the yo with the next and the previous stitch, turn work.

ROW 4 (WS): yo, p until 1 st before previous yo remains, p3tog the yo with the next and the previous stitch, turn work.

Repeat rows 3 and 4 — 17 (20, 23, 26, 29, 34) times more.

DIVIDE FOR BODY AND SLEEVES

(RS): yo, k to m, *remove m, place stitches before next marker on holder/waste yarn for sleeve, sm, k to m; repeat once from *, k until 1 st before previous yo remains, sssk the yo with the next and the previous stitch, turn work.

You have now 52 (56, 60, 65, 70, 80) sts on each holder for sleeves and 76 (86, 96, 106, 116, 126) sts on the needle between side markers for the back.

Body

Continue even in short rows working in St st as follows – on RS: yo, k until 1 st before previous yo remains, sssk the yo with the next and the previous st, turn work; on WS: yo, p until 1 st before previous yo remains, p3tog the yo with the next and the previous st, turn work. When body measures 2″ [5 cm] from underarm, begin waist shaping —

DECREASE ROW (RS): yo, k until 6 sts before m remain, k2tog, k to m, sm, k4, ssk; repeat once from *, k until 1 st before previous yo remains, sssk the yo with the next and the previous st, turn work.

Repeat the decrease row 3 more times every 4th row. Work even as established additional 2″ [5 cm].

INCREASE ROW (RS): yo, k until 5 sts before m remain, m1R, k to m, sm, k5, m1L; repeat once from *, k until 1 st before previous yo remains, sssk the yo with the next and the previous stitch, turn work.

Repeat the increase row 3 times more on every 4th row and after that 4 times more every 6th row. Continue even in St st and short rows as established until 26 sts of front band sts remain. Work in 1×1 rib until all front band sts are used up. BO sts loosely in 1×1 rib.

Sleeves

Note: You can pick a few extra stitches from the underarm for all sizes to prevent hole – or sew the gap while finishing the garment. Decrease these extra picked up stitches on next possible round.

Place the 52 (56, 60, 65, 70, 80) sts of sleeve from holder on smaller dpns. Pm to indicate beginning of the round and join yarn. Work even in St st until the sleeve measures 2″ [5 cm] from underarm. Start decreases on next round.

DECREASE ROUND: k2, ssk, k until 4 sts remain, k2tog, k to end.

Repeat the decrease round 2 (2, 2, 3, 3, 3) times more every 2″ [5 cm]. Work even St st until sleeve measures 10″ [26 cm]. *Size L only*: k2tog the first st on next round. *All sizes*: Continue in 1×1 rib for an additional 5″ [12 cm]. BO sts loosely in rib.

Finishing

Weave in all yarn ends. Sew the pockets on WS. Wet block the cardigan to measurements.

Stripe & Cable

Sweet cables and raspberry red stripes — just what mittens should look like! It's like Rustic Aarni yarn is meant for these lovely striped mittens.

Materials

Yarn

2 skeins of Aarni by Riihivilla (100% Finnsheep wool; 230 yards [210 meters]/ 100g), one skein in each color. Approx. 130 yards [120 meters] of MC and 90 yards [80 meters] of CC. The sample was knit using two hallon shaded red colorways.

Needles

US 4 [3.5 mm] and US 1½ [2.5 mm] dpns. Adjust needle size if necessary to obtain the correct gauge.

Notions

Stitch markers, cable needle, tapestry needle and blocking aids.

Sizing

One size

Hand circumference of mitten: 7¾" [20 cm].

Gauge

20 sts and 34 rnds = 4" [10 cm] in garter stitch using larger needles.

Chart A

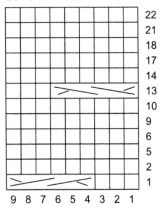

9 8 7 6 5 4 3 2 1

22
21
18
17
14
13
10
9
6
5
2
1

Chart Key

Slip 3 sts on cable needle and hold on WS of the work, k3, k3 from cable needle.

Slip 3 sts on cable needle and hold on RS of the work, k3, k3 from cable needle.

☐ Knit.

Note: Read the chart from right to left. Only MC rounds are shown on chart.

Right Mitten

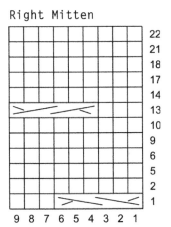

9 8 7 6 5 4 3 2 1

22
21
18
17
14
13
10
9
6
5
2
1

Mitten

Using smaller needles CO 40 sts. Divide evenly on dpns, pm for beg of rnd and join in round. Work 1″ in 2×2 ribbing.

Change to larger dpns and work 2″ [5 cm] in garter st with 2-row stripes in each color and place cable on first rnd (MC, knit rnd; *Right mitten/ Left mitten*): k 4/ 27, work row 1 of chart A, k to end of rnd. Work 2″ [5 cm] as established 2-row stripes in garter st and work through chart A on cable stitches (slip the cable stitches on both CC rnds).

INCREASE FOR THUMB

MC, K ROUND (*Right mitten/ Left mitten*): work *19/21* sts, pm, m1R, k1, m1L, pm, work to end of rnd. Work the inc round every knit MC rnds for 3 more

times: work to m, sm, m1R, k to m, m1L, sm, k to end [*48 sts*]. Work 1″ [2.5 cm] as established 2-row stripes in garter st and work through chart A on cable stitches — end with MC rnds. Transfer thumb stitches on holder: k to m, remove m, place the next 9 sts on holder, remove m and CO 1 st using backwrads-loop CO, k to end of rnd [*40 sts*].

Work additional 4″ [10 cm] as established with 2-row stripes in garter st and work through chart A on cable stitches. Continue in St st in MC only and begin decreases: ssk, k16, k2tog, pm, ssk, k16, k2tog. Work decreases on every rnd until 14 sts remain: *ssk, k until 2 sts before m remain, k2tog, sm; repeat once from *.

Divide remaining sts evenly on two dpns, turn mitten inside out with WS facing and BO using three-needle BO.

Thumb

Place held sts on larger dpns and join MC yarn. Pick up and knit 3 sts around the CO st, pm for beg of rnd and join in rnd [*12 sts*]. K until thumb measures 2″ [5 cm]. Begin decreases —

DECREASE RND 1: *k2, k2tog; repeat from * to end of rnd.

DECREASE RND 2: *k1, k2tog; repeat from * to end of rnd.

DECREASE RND 3: *k2tog; repeat from * to end of rnd.

Cut yarn and thread trough remaining stitches twice, pull tight to close the hole and fasten on WS.

Finishing

Weave in all yarn ends and block the mittens using your preferred method.

Yellow

YELLOW IS ONE OF THE THREE PRIMARY COLORS AND IN NATURAL DYEING THIS
REALLY IS THE CASE — YELLOW DYES HAVE BEEN THE MOST EASY TO FIND,
ALMOST EVERYWHERE. IN NATURAL DYEING COMMON SOURCES FOR YELLOW DYES
HAVE BEEN WELD, OR DYER'S WEED, WOUNDWORT AND SAFFLOWER. YELLOW
BANDAGES DYED USING SAFFLOWER HAVE BEEN FOUND ON EGYPTIAN MUMMIES.

YELLOW is often associated with the sun or with gold. Those words are also etymologically related; both of them appear to derive from Indo-European word *ghel*. The Arabic word for yellow is *zafran* and that is the base for word *saffron*. The name refers to both the plant as the orange-yellow color.

Saffron has been used in dyeing also: some findings have been made from Greek ruins and it is also mentioned as a dye in the Bible. Mainly, though, saffron has always been a valuable plant used sparingly as spice.

In many Eastern cultures yellow has been a particularly valuable color, especially in China. It's the color of wisdom and happiness. In Europe the color also has negative connotations, sometimes associated with treachery, cowardice or corruption. One origin of this could be seen in medieval Christian art, when deceitful Judas Iscariot was often portrayed in yellow robes.

Nowadays, the strongest associations of yellow and orange are joy and cheerfulness.

Bric-a-Brac

Bric-a-Brac is a cowl and beanie set, just perfect for keeping you warm in the coldest days of the year. The set is worked with playful short rows and reverse colors for a super fun knitting experience.

Materials

Yarn

2 (2) skeins of Helmi by Rintalan Luomutila (100% wool; 185 yds [170 m] per 100 g), one skein in each color. Approx. 315 (370) yards [290 (340) meters] of DK weight yarn. Sample was knit in the colorways yellow (MC) and gray (CC) and in size large.

Needles

US 7 [4 mm] and US 4 [3.5 mm] circular needles; 16˝ [40 cm] long, and US 7 [4 mm] dpns. Adjust needle size if necessary to obtain the correct gauge.

Notions

A stitch marker, tapestry needle, blocking aids.

Sizing

Adult's S (L)

Finished circumference of the cowl: 20 (22)˝ [50 (56) cm] in circumference at top and 27 (29)˝ [68 (74) cm] at bottom.

Finished measurements of the beanie: 17¾ (19½)˝ [45 (49) cm] at the brim.

Gauge

18 sts and 26 rows = 4˝ [10 cm] Stockinette stitch using larger needle.

Stitch Pattern

Twisted Ribbing (in the round)
*k1 tbl, p1; repeat from * to end of rnd.

Cowl

Using smaller circ needle and MC, CO 90 (100) sts. Join in round, carefully not twisting your stitches. Pm for beg of rnd and for the middle of rnd, after 45 (50) sts. Work in twisted ribbing until the piece measures 1¼" [3 cm]. Change to larger needle and continue 3 rnds in St st. Increase on next round: *k2, m1L, k until two sts before m remain, m1R, k2, sm; repeat once from *.

First set of short rows

Short row 1 (RS): k 44 (49), turn work.

Short row 2 (WS): yo, p 43 (48), turn work.

Short row 3 (RS): yo, k until 4 sts before previous yo remain, turn work.

Short row 4 (WS): yo, p until 4 sts before previous yo remain, turn work.

Repeat short rows 3 and 4 two more times. After last repeat of row 4, work a yarn-over, k to end of round picking up first set of yo's (k2tog each yo with the next st). On next round pick up the remaining yo's (ssk the yo's with the previous st). Work an increase round as established and start striping on next round: knit one round with CC, one with MC, repeat 5 more times (until you have 6 stripes of CC). Change to MC and work an increase round. Work two rounds in St st.

Second set of short rows

Short row 5 (RS): k 22 (25) sts past middle marker, turn work.

Short row 6 (WS): yo, p 43 (48), turn work.

Short row 7 (RS): yo, k until 4 sts before previous yo remain, turn work.

Short row 8 (WS): yo, p until 4 sts before previous yo remain, turn work.

Repeat short rows 7 and 8 two more times. After last repeat of row 8, work a yarn-over, k to end of round picking up first set of yo's (k2tog each yo with the next st). On next round pick up the remaining yo's (ssk the yo's with the previous st). Work an increase round as established and start striping on next round: knit one round with CC, one with MC, repeat 5 more times (until you have 6 stripes of CC). Change to MC and work an increase round. Work two rounds in St st.

Third set of short rows

Short row 9 (RS): k until 1 st of round remains, turn work.

Short row 10 (WS): yo, p 43 (48), turn work.

Short row 11 (RS): yo, k until 4 sts before previous yo remain, turn work.

Short row 12 (WS): yo, p until 4 sts before previous yo remain, turn work.

Repeat short rows 11 and 12 two more times. After last repeat of row 12, work a yarn-over, k to end of round picking up first set of yo's (k2tog each yo with the next st). On next round pick up the remaining yo's (ssk the yo's with the previous st). Work an increase round as established and start striping on the next round: knit one round with CC, one with MC, repeat 5 more times (until you have 6 stripes of CC). Change to MC and work an increase round. Work two rounds in St st.

Fourth set of short rows

Short row 13 (RS): k 22 (25), turn work.

Short row 14 (WS): yo, p 43 (48), turn work.

Short row 15 (RS): yo, k until 4 sts before previous yo remain, turn work.

Short row 16 (WS): yo, p until 4 sts before previous yo remain, turn work.

Repeat short rows 15 and 16 two more times. After last repeat of row 16, work a yarn-over, k to end of round picking up first set of yo's (k2tog each yo with the next st). On next round pick up the remaining yo's (ssk the yo's with the previous st). Work an increase

round as established [after all increase rounds you have 122 (132) sts on needle]. Change to smaller needle and work in twisted ribbing until the piece measures 1¼" [3 cm]. BO sts loosely in twisted ribbing.

Beanie

Using smaller circ needle and CC, CO 80 (88) sts. Join in round, carefully not twisting your stitches. Pm for beg of rnd and middle of rnd, after 40 (44) sts. Work in twisted ribbing until the piece measures 1¼" [3 cm]. Change to larger circ needle and work two rounds in St st.

First set of short rows

Short row 1 (RS): k 39 (43), turn work.

Short row 2 (WS): yo, p 38 (42), turn work.

Short row 3 (RS): yo, k until 3 sts before previous yo remain, turn work.

Short row 4 (WS): yo, p until 3 sts before previous yo remain, turn work.

Repeat short rows 3 and 4 two more times. After last repeat of row 4, work a yarn-over, k to end of round picking up first set of yo's (k2tog each yo with the next st). On next round pick up the remaining yo's (ssk the yo's with the previous st). Start striping on next round: knit one round with MC, one with CC, repeat 3 more times (until you have 4 stripes of MC). Change to CC and work two rounds in St st.

Second set of short rows

Short row 5 (RS): k 59 (65), turn work.

Short row 6 (WS): yo, p 38 (42), turn work.

Short row 7 (RS): yo, k until 3 sts before previous yo remain, turn work.

Short row 8 (WS): yo, p until 3 sts before previous yo remain, turn work.

Repeat short rows 7 and 8 two more times. After last repeat of row 8, work a yarn-over, k to end of round picking up first set of yo's (k2tog each yo with the next st). On next round pick up the remaining yo's with the previous st). Start striping on next round: knit one round with MC, one with CC, repeat 3 more times (until you have 4 stripes of MC). Change to CC and work two rounds in St st.

Third set of short rows

Short row 9 (RS): k 22 (25) sts past middle marker, turn work.

Short row 10 (WS): yo, p 38 (42), turn work.

Short row 11 (RS): yo, k until 3 sts before previous yo remain, turn work.

Short row 12 (WS): yo, p until 3 sts before previous yo remain, turn work.

Repeat short rows 11 and 12 two more times. After last repeat of row 12, work a yarn-over, k to end of round picking up first set of yo's (k2tog each yo with the next st). On next round pick up the remaining yo's (ssk the yo's with the previous st). Start striping on next round: knit one round with MC, one with CC, repeat 3 more times (until you have 4 stripes of MC). Change to CC and work two rounds in St st.

Begin decreases — *note: continue in CC only and change to dpns when necessary.*

Setup decrease round: *k 8 (9), k2tog, pm; repeat from * yo end of rnd.

Decrease round: *k until 2 sts before m remain, k2tog; repeat from * to end of rnd.

Repeat decrease round until 8 sts remain. Cut yarn and thread through remaining stitches twice. Pull tight to cover the hole and fasten on the WS.

Finishing

Weave in all yarn ends. Block the cowl and beanie to measurements using your preferred method.

Color Block

Color Block is a happy tunic worked from top down with raglan shaping. Subtle short-row shaping at the neck, a spot of contrast color at the hem and an A-line shape are the key factors in this tunic.

Materials

Yarn

3 (4, 4, 5, 5) skeins of Aada by Hopeasäie (100% superwash merino: 181 yds [166 m] per skein). Approx. 360 (440, 520, 600, 670, 720) yards [330 (400, 480, 550, 610, 660) meters] of MC and 50 (50, 60, 60, 70, 70) yards [45 (45, 55, 55, 65, 65) meters] of CC. Sample was knit in the colorways Vanha Roosa (MC) and Kesäloma (CC): in size 12 years.

Needles

US 9 [5.5 mm] circular needles, 24″ [60 cm] long, and dpns. Adjust needle size if necessary to obtain the correct gauge.

Notions

Two 1″ [2.5 cm] buttons, tapestry needle, stitch markers, stitch holders/waste yarn and blocking aids.

Sizing

2 (4, 6, 8, 10, 12) Years

Finished chest circumference: 23 (25, 27, 29, 31, 33)″ [58 (62, 67, 72, 78, 82) cm]. Choose a size with a small amount of positive ease.

Gauge

16 sts and 26 rows = 4″ [10 cm] in Stockinette stitch.

Finished measurements

17 (17½, 18½, 19, 20½, 21½)″
[42 (44, 46, 48, 52, 54) cm]

8 (8½, 9, 9½, 10, 10½)″
[20 (21, 22, 24, 25, 27) cm]

4 (5, 5½, 6, 7, 7¾)″
[10 (12, 13, 15, 15, 19) cm]

15 (16, 16½, 17, 18, 19)″
[38 (40, 42, 44, 46, 48) cm]

23 (25, 27, 29, 31, 33)″
[58 (62, 67, 72, 78, 82) cm]

Collar

Using circ needle and MC, CO 76 (78, 82, 84, 90, 94) sts. Do not join. Work 1″ [2.5 cm] in garter st (back and forth). End with WS row. Work first buttonhole on next row (RS): k4, yo, k2tog, k to end. Continue with back of the neck increases on next RS row: k10, *kfb, k1; repeat 8 times from *, k until 28 sts remain, *k1, kfb; repeat 8 times from *, k to end [94 (96, 100, 102, 108, 112) sts on needle]. Work three more rows in garter st.

Shape neck with short rows —

SHORT ROWS 1 AND 2 (RS and WS): k 14, W&T; k to end.

SHORT ROWS 3 AND 4 (RS and WS): k 4 sts past previous wrapped st, W&T; k to end.

Repeat short rows 3 and 4 — 3 (3, 4, 4, 5, 5) times more. Knit to end on next row (RS). Work short rows to left end —

SHORT ROWS 6 AND 7 (WS and RS): k 14, W&T; k to end.

SHORT ROWS 8 AND 9 (WS and RS): k 4 sts past previous wrapped st, W&T; k to end.

Repeat short rows 8 and 9 — 3 (3, 4, 4, 5, 5) times more. Knit to end on next row (WS). Work second button-hole as established. Continue in garter st until the collar measures 2″ [5 cm] at the front (shallowest part).

Yoke

Join in round — Place the last 8 sts on one dpn and hold parallel at back of the left circ needle. Pm for beg of round and k2tog using one st from each needle until all sts from dpn are used up [86 (88, 92, 94, 100, 104) sts remain]. Continue with raglan increases working in St st —

SETUP ROUND: k 7 (7, 8, 9, 10, 11), pm, k14, pm, k 29 (30, 32, 33, 36, 38), pm, k 14, pm, k to end.

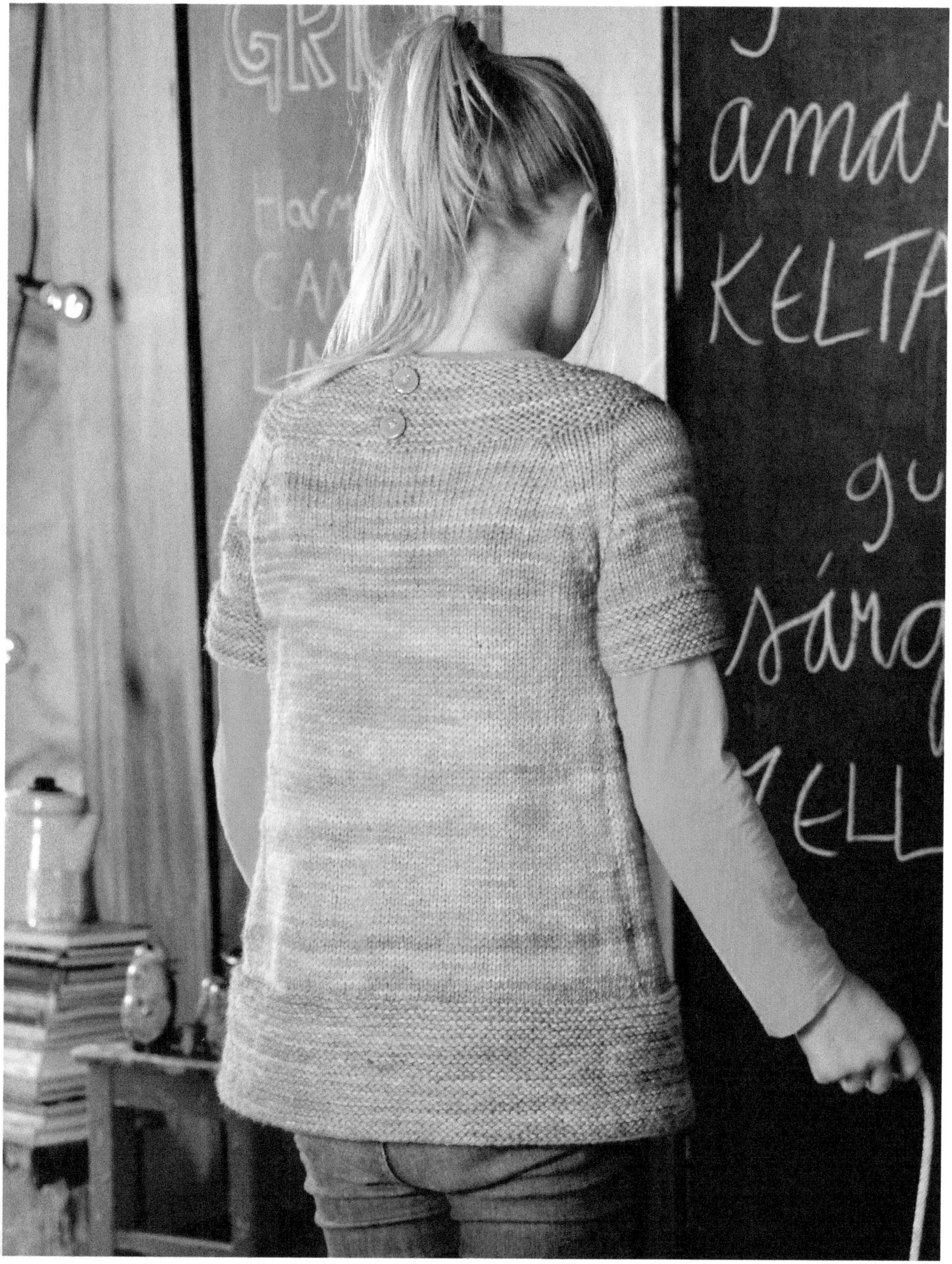

Round 1 (increase rnd): sm, *k until 2 sts before m remain, m1R, k2, sm, k2, m1R; repeat three more times from *, k to end of rnd.

Round 2: k to end slipping markers.

Repeat rounds 1 and 2 – 8 (9, 10, 11, 12, 13) times more.

Divide for body and sleeves

Sm, *k to m, remove m, place all sts before next m on holder for sleeve, sm; repeat once from *, k to end.

You have now 32 (34, 36, 38, 40, 42) sts on each holder for the sleeves and 94 (100, 108, 114, 124, 132) sts on the needle for the body.

Body

Continue even working St st in MC. When the body measures 2 (2, 2, 3, 3, 3)″ [5 (5, 5, 8, 8, 8) cm] from underarm, begin increases —

Increase round: sm, *k until 4 sts before m remain, m1L, k to m, sm, k4, m1R, repeat once from *, k to end.

Repeat the increase round every 1½″ [4 cm] until the tunic measures 10 (11, 11½, 12, 13, 14)″ [26 (28, 30, 32, 34, 36) cm] from underarm. Cut yarn and place 24 (24, 26, 26, 28, 28) stitches to left from middle of the front on holder.

Hem

Join yarn to remaining sts on needle, beginning from the middle of the front (RS) and knit to end (to held sts of front). Work back and forth in garter st until the garter st hem measures 5″ [12 cm]. BO hem sts.

Color Block

Change to CC. Place the held sts on one dpn. Working with circ needle, pick up and knit 20 sts sideways from the left side of the MC garter st hem RS facing (or approx. one st every two rows). Work in garter st and ssk the last st of row together with the next st on dpn on each RS row. Work as established until all sts on dpn are worked up and the sideways piece reaches the middle end on MC garter hem. BO the CC sts.

Sleeves

Note: You can pick a few extra stitches from the underarm for all sizes to prevent hole – or sew the gap while finishing the garment. Decrease these extra picked up stitches on next possible round.

Place the 32 (34, 36, 38, 40, 42) sts of sleeve from holder on smaller dpns. Pm to indicate beginning of the round and join MC yarn to underarm. Work even in St st until the sleeve measures 1 (1, 1, 1½, 1½, 2)″ [2.5 (2.5, 2.5, 4, 4, 5) cm] from underarm. Work 2″ [5 cm] in garter st. BO sts loosely.

Finishing

Weave in all yarn ends. Sew on buttons to the back and seam the BO edge color block to MC garter hem. Block the tunic to measurements using your preferred method.

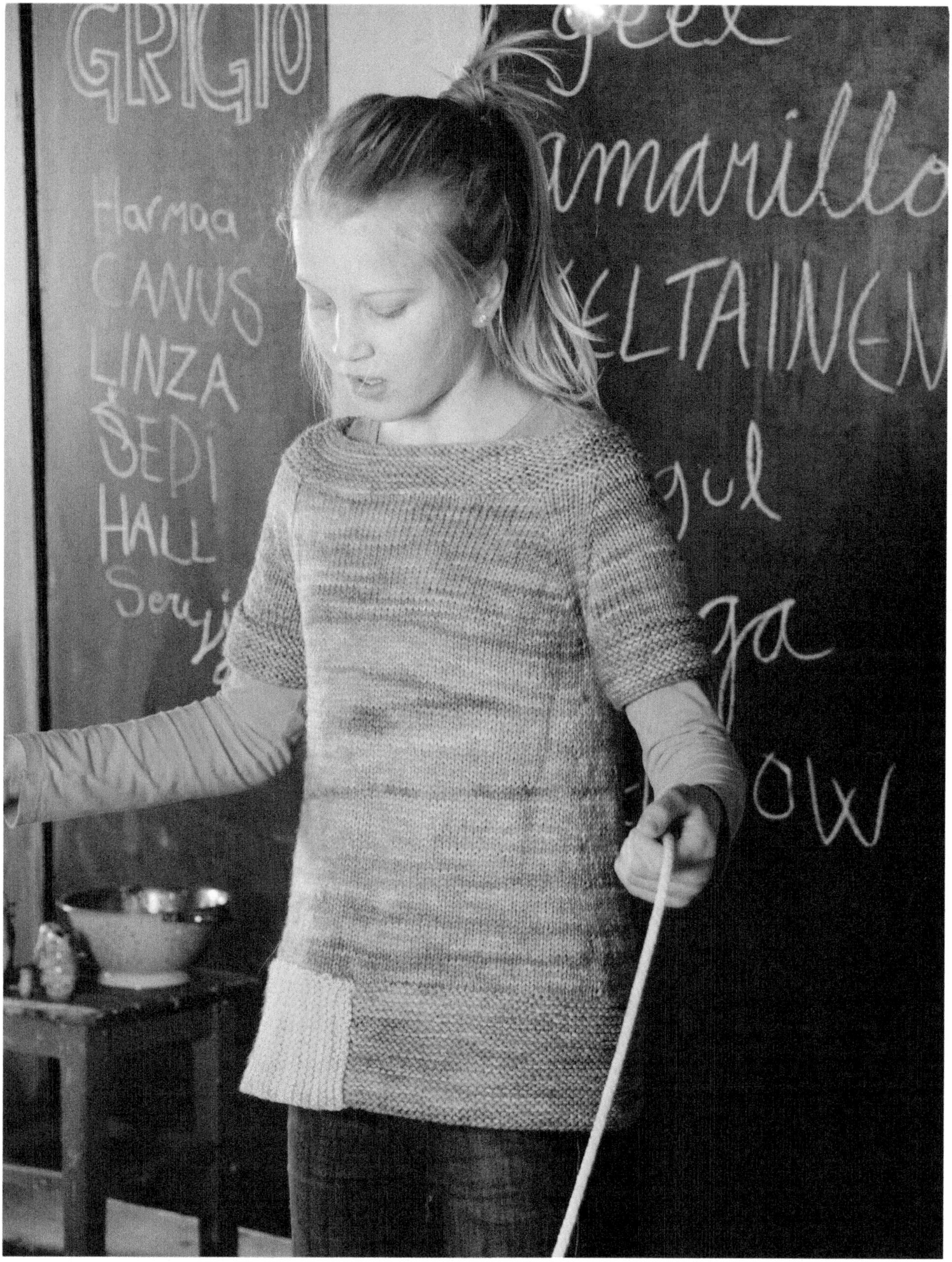
GRIGIO
Harmaa
CANUS
LINZA
HALL

Button Back

Button Back is a trusted sweater with a modern twist, just what every kid needs. It has a warm funnel neck, playful stripes and little pockets.

Materials

Yarn

3 (3, 4, 5, 5) skeins of Sweater by The Plucky Knitter (90% merino, 10% nylon; 270 yds [247 m] per skein). Approx. 420 (490, 540, 660, 800) yards [380 (450, 490, 600, 730) meters] of MC and 220 (260, 310, 380, 460) yards [200 (240, 280, 340, 420) meters] of CC. Sample was knit in the colorways Dandy Lion (MC) and Sticky Toffee (CC); in size 6 years.

Needles

US 6 [4 mm] and US 2½ [3 mm] circular needles, 24″ [60 cm] long, and dpns. Adjust needle size if necessary to obtain the correct gauge.

Notions

Three 1″ [2.5 cm] buttons, tapestry needle, stitch markers, stitch holders/waste yarn and blocking aids.

Sizing

2 (4, 6, 8, 10, 12) Years

Finished chest circumference: 23 (25, 27, 29, 31, 33)″ [58 (62, 67, 72, 78, 82) cm]. Choose a size with a small amount of positive ease.

Gauge

18 sts and 26 rows = 4″ [10 cm] in Stockinette stitch using larger needle.

Finished measurements

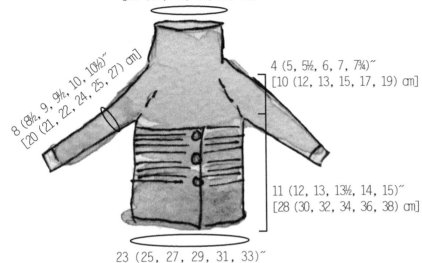

16 (17, 18, 20, 21, 22)″
[40 (42, 46, 52, 56) cm]

8 (8½, 9, 9½, 10, 10½)″
[20 (21, 22, 24, 25, 27) cm]

4 (5, 5½, 6, 7, 7¾)″
[10 (12, 13, 15, 17, 19) cm]

11 (12, 13, 13½, 14, 15)″
[28 (30, 32, 34, 36, 38) cm]

23 (25, 27, 29, 31, 33)″
[58 (62, 67, 72, 78, 82) cm]

Collar

Using smaller dpns and MC, CO 72 (76, 82, 90, 96, 100) sts – or use smaller circ needle with magic loop. Join in round, pm for beginning of round and work two rounds in St st. Continue in twisted rib until the piece measures 1″ [2.5 cm]. Change to larger dpns/circ needle and work in St st until the collar measures 4″ [10 cm].

Yoke

Continue with raglan increases in St st with MC and shape the neck with short rows —

SETUP SHORT ROW (RS): k 6 (7, 8, 9, 11, 12), m1R, k2, pm, k2, m1R, k 6 (6, 6, 8, 8, 8), m1R, k2, pm, k2, m1L, k1, turn work.

SETUP SHORT ROW (WS): yo, p to last m (beg of rnd), sm, p 16 (17, 19, 20, 21, 22), m1L (purl), p2, pm, p2, m1R (purl), p 6 (6, 6, 8, 8, 8), m1L (purl), p2, pm, p2, p1, turn work.

SHORT ROW 1 (RS): yo, k to third m (beg of rnd), sm, *k until 2 sts before m remain, m1R, k2, sm, k2, m1R; repeat once from *, k to previous yo, k2tog the yo with the next st, turn work.

SHORT ROW 2 (WS): yo, p to third m (beg of rnd), sm, *p until 2 sts before m remain, m1L (purl), p2, sm, p2, m1R (purl); repeat once from *, p to previous yo, ssp the yo with the next st, turn work.

Repeat short rows 1 and 2 — 3 (4, 4, 5, 5, 6) times more. Work to end of rnd after last WS row: yo, k to third m (beg of rnd), sm.

Continue raglan increases — *Note: Pick up the last yarn-overs on first raglan increase rounds, k2tog the first yo with the next stitch and ssk the second with previous stitch.*

ROUND 1 (increase rnd): sm, *k until 2 sts before m remain, m1R, k2, sm, k2, m1R; repeat three more times from *, k to end of rnd.

ROUND 2: k to end slipping markers.

Repeat rounds 1 and 2 – 7 (7, 8, 8, 9, 9) times more.

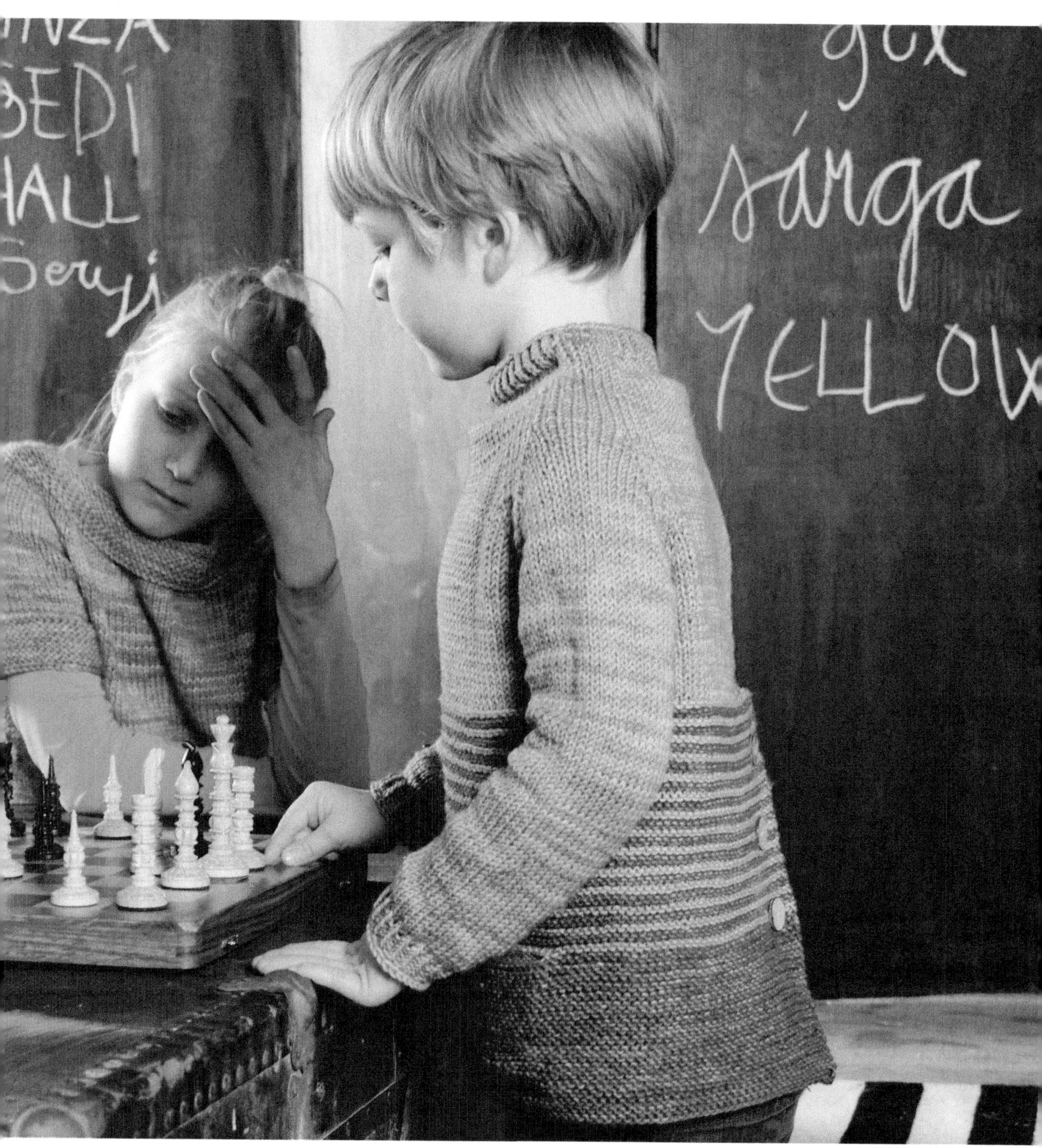
sárga

Divide for Body and Sleeves

Sm, *k to m, remove m, place all sts before next m on holder for sleeve, remove m; repeat once from *, k to end.

You have now 36 (38, 40, 44, 46, 48) sts on each holder for sleeves and 104 (112, 122, 130, 140, 148) sts on the needle for the body.

Body

Continue even working St st in MC. When the body measures 2 (2, 2, 3, 3, 3)" [5 (5, 5, 8, 8, 8) cm] from underarm, start working back and forth in garter st and begin striping as follows (MC and WS): remove m and turn your work, k to end, CO 10 sts using backward-loop cast-on method [*114 (122, 132, 140, 150, 158) sts on the needle*]. Change to CC and knit two rows. Continue working two-row stripes with MC and CC. When you are working fourth row in CC (RS) work first buttonhole: k until 7 sts remain, ssk, yo, k to end. Continue striping and repeat the buttonhole row every 2" [5 cm] for two more times.

Continue in CC only and place pockets on next RS row: k 34 (38, 43, 46, 50, 53), Place the next 15 sts on holder for pocket lining and CO 15 sts using backward-loop cast-on method, k 16 (16, 16, 18, 20, 22), place the next 15 sts on another holder for pocket lining and CO 15 sts using backward-loop cast-on method, k to end. Continue in garter st until the body measures 11 (12, 13, 13½, 14, 15)" [28 (30, 32, 34, 36, 38) cm] from underarm. BO sts loosely.

Sleeves

Note: You can pick a few extra stitches from the underarm for all sizes to prevent hole – or sew the gap while finishing the garment. Decrease these extra picked up stitches on next possible round.

Place the 36 (38, 40, 44, 46, 48) sts of sleeve from holder on smaller dpns. Pm to indicate beginning of the round and join yarn to underarm. Work even in St st until the sleeve measures 2" [5 cm] from underarm.

Decrease round: k2, ssk, k until 4 sts remain, k2tog, k to end.

Repeat the decrease round 3 times more every 3" [8 cm]. Work even in St st until sleeve measures 8½ (9½, 10½, 12, 13, 13½)" [22 (24, 26, 30, 32, 34) cm]. Change to smaller dpns and work 1" [2.5 cm] in twisted ribbing. Work two rounds in St st. BO sts loosely in rib.

Pockets

Place the 15 held sts on one dpn and join yarn (MC). Work in rev St st and increase one st on both ends on first row (WS): k1, m1R, k until 1 st remains, m1L, k1. Work even in rev St st until the pocket lining nearly reaches hem (approx. 1" [2.5 cm] less than the body length). BO lining sts.

Finishing

Weave in all yarn ends. Sew on buttons to the back and pocket linings to WS. Block the sweater to measurements using your preferred method.

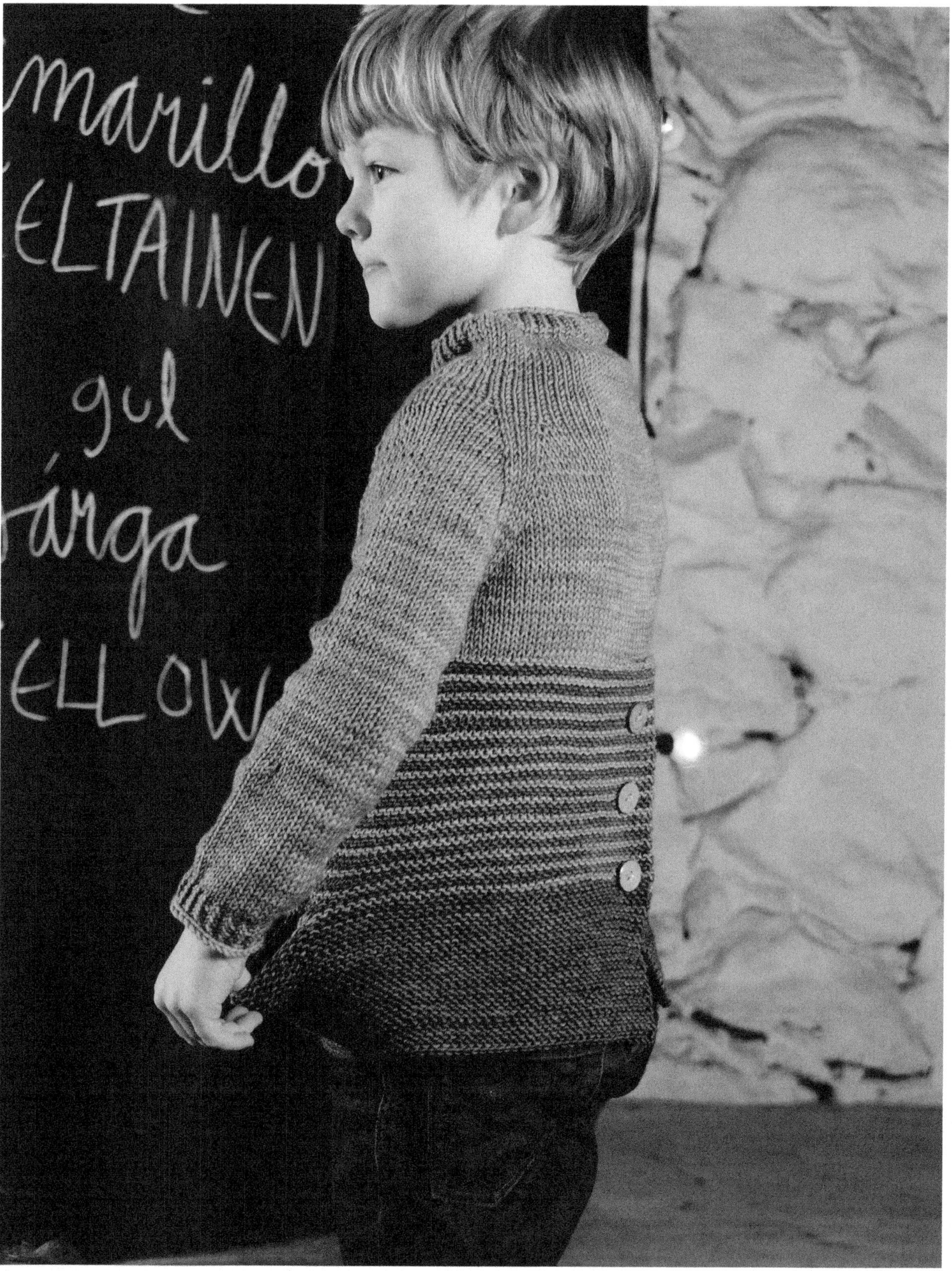
marillo
ELTAINEN
gul
árga
ELLOW

Knit & Purl

KNIT & PURL MITTENS WILL KEEP YOUR HANDS WARM ON THE BRISKEST WINTER DAYS. ALTERNATING STOCKINETTE AND REVERSE STOCKINETTE STITCH HIGHLIGHTS THE SUBTLE TONE CHANGES IN THIS PLANT-DYED YARN.

Materials

YARN

1 skein of plant-dyed yarn by Rintalan Luomutila (100% Finn-sheep wool). Approx. 225 yards [200 meters] of DK weight yarn. Sample was knit in size Men.

NEEDLES

US 6 [4 mm] and US 2½ [3 mm] dpns. Adjust needle size if necessary to obtain the correct gauge.

NOTIONS

Tapestry needle, stitch markers and blocking aids.

Sizing

WOMEN (MEN)

Mitten circumference: 7½ (8½)″ [19 (22) cm].

Gauge

18 sts and 26 rounds = 4″ [10 cm] in Stockinette stitch using larger needles.

Mitten

Using smaller needles CO 34 (40) sts. Divide evenly on dpns, pm for beg of rnd and join in round. Work 1¾" in 1X1 ribbing.

Change to larger dpns and work 2" in St st and rev St st as follows (*Right mitten/ Left mitten*): k *19 (22)/2 (2)*, p 13 (16), k to end of rnd.

INCREASE FOR THUMB

Right mitten/ Left mitten: work as established *0 (0)/33 (39)* sts, m1R, pm, k1, pm, m1L, work to end of rnd. Work increase round on every second rnd 4 (5) times more: work to m, m1R, sm, k1, sm, m1L, work to end of rnd [*46 (54) sts*]. Work 1" [2,5 cm] as established. Transfer thumb stitches on holder (*Right mitten/ Left mitten*): work as established *0 (0)/33 (39)* sts, place the next 11 (13) sts on holder and at the same time remove markers, CO 1 st using backward-loop CO and work to end of rnd as established [*34 (40) sts*].

Work 4 (4¾)" [10 (12) cm] in St st and rev St st as established: knit *19 (22)/ 2 (2)* sts, purl 13 (16), k to end of rnd. Work 3 rnds in St st. Begin decreases: ssk, k 13 (16), k2tog, pm, ssk, k 13 (16), k2tog. Decrease on every rnd until 14 (12) sts remain: *ssk, k until 2 sts before m remain, k2tog, sm; repeat from * once.

Divide remaining stst evenly on two dpns, turn mitten inside out with WS facing and BO using three-needle BO.

Thumb

Place held sts on larger dpns and join yarn. Pick up and knit 3 sts around the CO st, pm for beg of rnd and join in rnd [*14 (16) sts*]. Work in St st until thumb measures 2 (2¼)" [5 (6) cm]. Begin decreases —

DECREASE RND 1: *k2, k2tog; repeat from * to end of rnd.

DECREASE RND 2: *k1, k2tog; repeat from * to end of rnd.

DECREASE RND 3: work k2tog to end of rnd.

Cut yarn and thread through remaining stitches twice, pull tight to close the hole and fasten on WS.

Finishing

Weave in all yarn ends and block the mittens using your preferred method.

Gray and Brown

In many color theories both gray and brown are a bit hard to place. Gray is considered to be a blend of colorless colors, black and white. Brown on the other hand is hardly at all a spectral hue but merely a pigment.

Gray

like a silver arrow

Though for a knitter, gray is real treasure. Bare eye can distinguish up to a few hundred shades of gray – so there really is plenty to choose from! Gray can be appreciated as a neutral ground or background color for all other colors. Also gray shades give space for the interplay between light and shadow. Even the black-and white photography is mostly dominated by shades of gray, rather than pure black or white.

Before the development of synthetic dyes, gray yarn and fabrics were most often obtained by the same dyes that were used for black.

One of the most important sources of natural black is the heartwood of a tree called logwood. The same tree provides amazing amount of different colors – everything from navy blue to red, purple and lavender – depending on what sort of mordant you use.

Natural brown dyes are often obtained from particular trees. In knitting and yarn produce, more common has been brown wool in natural color, brown from black sheep. Lighter browns have been created by blending wool from white and black sheep.

Skyline

THE CLEAN LINES OF THE 60'S AND THE EVER-FASHIONABLE SAILOR STYLE INSPIRED THIS UNCOMPLICATED TUNIC. THE TUNIC IS WORKED FROM THE TOP DOWN IN ONE PIECE, FEATURING A CUTE BOAT NECK AND ¾ SLEEVES.

Materials

YARN

3 (4, 4, 4, 4, 5) skeins of Silky Merino Fingering by The Uncommon Thread (75% Merino, 25% Silk; 440 yds [402 m]/100g). Approx. 1300 (1400, 1520, 1630, 1750, 1850) yards [1190 (1280, 1390, 1490, 1600, 1700) meters] of fingering weight yarn). Sample was knit in the colorway Nimbostratus in size small.

NEEDLES

US 4 [3.5 mm] and US 2½ [3 mm] circular needles and dpns. Adjust needle size if necessary to obtain the correct gauge.

NOTIONS

Tapestry needle, stitch markers, stitch holders/waste yarn and blocking aids.

Sizing

XS (S, M, L, XL, XXL)

Finished chest circumference: 30 (34, 38, 42, 46, 50)″ [75 (85, 95, 105, 115, 125) cm]. The tunic is intended to be worn with no ease.

Gauge

24 sts and 32 rounds = 4″ [10 cm] in Stockinette stitch using larger needles.

Finished measurements

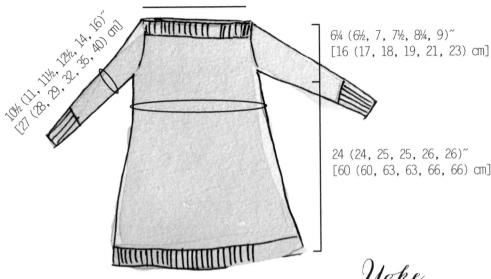

12 (13, 15, 16, 17, 18)˝
30 (33, 36, 40, 43, 46) cm

6¼ (6½, 7, 7½, 8¼, 9)˝
[16 (17, 18, 19, 21, 23) cm]

10½ (11, 11½, 12½, 14, 16)˝
[27 (28, 29, 32, 35, 40) cm]

24 (24, 25, 25, 26, 26)˝
[60 (60, 63, 63, 66, 66) cm]

30 (34, 38, 42, 46, 50)˝
[75 (85, 95, 105, 115, 125) cm]

Collar

BACK OF COLLAR

Using smaller circular needle, CO 72 (78, 88, 98, 106, 112) sts. Do not join in round. Work in 1×1 twisted ribbing until the piece measures 3″ [8 cm]. Break yarn and leave the sts on needle.

FRONT OF COLLAR

Using the same needle, CO 72 (78, 88, 98, 106, 112) sts. Do not join in round. Work in 1×1 twisted ribbing until the piece measures 3″ [8 cm].

You have now two separate pieces on the needle.

Yoke

JOIN COLLAR PIECES

(RS): Using larger circular needle and yarn attached to the second piece, place the front piece on top of the back piece (*right sides up on each piece and the live stitches of the front of the collar should point to opposite direction from the live stitches of the back*).

Place marker to indicate beginning of the round, pick up and knit 20 stitches from the narrow edge of the ribbed pieces (pick through both layers, front and back), pm, knit the back stitches (the back of the collar stitches on smaller needle), pm, pick up and knit 20 stitches from the other narrow edge of the ribbed pieces (pick through both layers, front and back), pm, k to end (the front of the collar stitches on smaller needle).

184 (196, 216, 236, 252, 264) sts on needle.

SHAPE THE NECK WITH SHORT ROWS

Note: You have joined sts in the round. The beginning of round is between front stitches and left sleeve stitches. To shape the boat neck, you will first work back and forth around left shoulder, then back and forth around right shoulder.

SETUP ROW 1 (RS): sm, m1L, k to m, m1R, sm, k6, turn work.

SETUP ROW 2 (WS): yo, p to m, sm, m1R (purl), p to m, m1L (purl), sm, p6, turn work.

SHORT ROW 1 (RS): yo, k to m, sm, m1L, k to m, m1R, sm, k to previous yo, k2tog the yo with the next st, turn work.

SHORT ROW 2 (WS): yo, p to m, sm, m1R (purl), p to m, m1L (purl), sm, p to previous yo, ssp the yo with the next st, turn work.

Repeat short rows 1 and 2 — 4 (4, 4, 5, 6, 8) times more.

CONTINUE WITH RIGHT SHOULDER INCREASES

SETUP ROW 1 (RS): yo, k to m, sm, *size xs only: m1L,* k to m, *size xs only: m1R,* sm, k to previous yo, k2tog the yo with the next st, k to m, sm, m1L, k to m, m1R, sm, k6, turn work.

SETUP ROW 2 (WS): yo, p to m, sm, m1R (purl), p to m, m1L (purl), sm, p6, turn work.

SHORT ROW 1 (RS): yo, k to m, sm, m1L, k to m, m1R, sm, k to previous yo, k2tog the yo with the next st, turn work.

SHORT ROW 2 (WS): yo, p to m, sm, m1R (purl), p to m, m1L (purl), sm, p to previous yo, ssp the yo with the next st, turn work.

Repeat short rows 1 and 2 — 4 (4, 4, 5, 6, 8) times more. Work to end of round as follows: yo, k to m, sm, *size xs only: m1R,* k to m, *size xs only: m1L,* sm, k to previous yo, k2tog the yo with the next st, k until 1 st before yo remain, ssk the yo with previous st, k to beg of round marker.

You have now 236 (244, 264, 292, 316, 344) sts and the last yarn-over on the needle.

Continue yoke working in the round without increases as follows – *Note: pick up the last yo on first round, ssk the yarn-over with previous stitch.*

ROUND 1: *sm, k to m, sm, slip the next st, k until 1 st before m remain, slip the next st; repeat once from *.

ROUND 2: *sm, k to m,; repeat 3 times from *.

Repeat rounds 1 and 2 until the piece measures 5 (5, 5, 5, 6, 6)″ [13 (13, 13, 13, 15, 15) cm] from shoulder, measure from the middle of the CO sleeve stitches edge on the collar and along slipped sts of sleeve seam. Begin increases for underarm:

ROUND 3 (increase round, body and sleeves): *sm, k2, m1L, k until 2 sts before m remain, m1R, k2; repeat 3 times from *.

ROUND 4: *sm, k to m,; repeat 3 times from *.

Repeat rounds 3 and 4 — 4 (6, 7, 8, 8, 10) times more.

SIZE XXL ONLY: Work rounds 5 and 6 once as follows —

ROUND 5 (increase round, body only): *sm, k to m, sm, k2, m1L, k until 2 sts before m remain, m1R, k2; repeat once from *.

ROUND 6: *sm, k to m,; repeat 3 times from *.

DIVIDE FOR BODY AND SLEEVES

*Remove marker, place the sts before next marker on holder for sleeve, CO 4 (5, 5, 5, 7, 7) sts using backward loop method, pm for side, CO another 4 (5, 5, 5, 7, 7) sts using backward loop method, remove m, k to m; repeat once from *.

You have now 56 (58, 60, 66, 70, 82) sts on each holder for sleeves and 180 (204, 228, 252, 276, 300) sts on the needle for the body.

Body

Continue in St st until the body measures 3″ [8 cm] from underarm.

INCREASE ROUND: * until 2 sts before m remain, m1R, k2, sm, k2, m1L; repeat once from *, k to end of round.

Repeat the increase round 8 times more every 2″ [5 cm] [*36 sts increased; 216 (240, 264, 288, 312, 336) sts on the needle*]. Continue even until the body measures 21 (21, 22, 22, 23, 23)″ [52 (52, 55, 55, 58, 58)

cm)]. Change to smaller circular needle. Continue in 1×1 twisted ribbing for additional 3″ [8 cm]. BO sts loosely in ribbing.

Sleeves

Place the 56 (58, 60, 66, 70, 82) sts of sleeve from holder on dpns. Join yarn and pick up and knit 4 (5, 5, 5, 7, 7) stitches from the middle of underarm CO edge, k 56 (58, 60, 66, 70, 82) and pick up and knit 4 (5, 5, 5, 7, 7) stitches from the other half of underarm CO edge [64 (68, 70, 76, 84, 96) sts on needles]. Pm to indicate beginning of the round and work even in St st until sleeve measures 2″ [5 cm].

DECREASE ROUND: k2, ssk, k until 4 sts remain, k2tog, k to end.

Repeat the decrease round 4 more times every 2″ [5 cm] [*10 sts decreased; 54 (58, 60, 66, 74, 86) sts remain*]. Continue in St st until the sleeve measures 11″ [28 cm].

Change to smaller dpns and continue in 1×1 twisted ribbing for additional 3″ [8 cm]. BO sleeve sts loosely in ribbing.

Finishing

Weave in all yarn ends. Wet block the tunic to measurements.

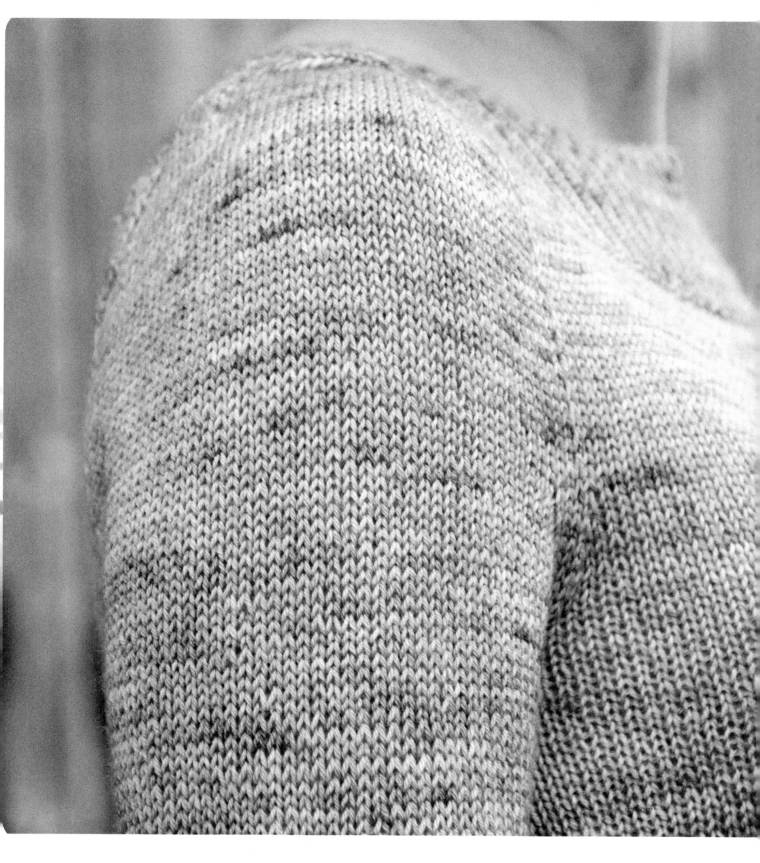

Freezing Point

Funky design meets easy knitting in this warm sweater for men. The patch details on the body and the sleeves add an edgy touch to this laid-back winter essential.

Materials

Yarn

7 (7, 8, 9, 10) skeins of Plucky Rustic by the Plucky Knitter (100% merino wool, 165 yds [151 m] per skein). Approx. 1040 (1155, 1270, 1385, 1500) yards [950 (1055, 1160, 1265, 1370) meters] of aran weight yarn. Sample was knit in the colorway Fisherman's Wharf and in size medium.

Needles

US 8 [5 mm] circular needles, 32″ [80 cm] long, and dpns. Adjust needle size if necessary to obtain the correct gauge.

Notions

Five 1″ [2.5 cm] buttons (or bigger), tapestry needle, stitch markers, stitch holders/waste yarn and blocking aids.

Sizing

S (M, L, XL, XXL)

Finished chest circumference: 36 (40, 44, 48, 52)″ [90 (100, 110, 120, 130 cm]. The sweater is intended to be worn with a few inches of positive ease.

Gauge

16 sts and 22 rows = 4″ [10 cm] in Stockinette stitch.

Finished Measurements

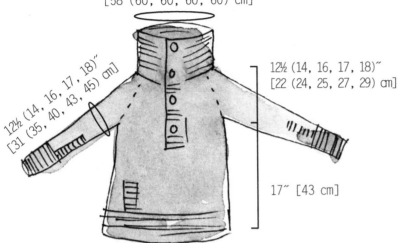

23 (24, 24, 24, 24)″
[58 (60, 60, 60, 60) cm]

12½ (14, 16, 17, 18)″
[22 (24, 25, 27, 29) cm]

12½ (14, 16, 17, 18)″
[31 (35, 40, 43, 45) cm]

17″ [43 cm]

Collar

36 (40, 44, 48, 52)″
[90 (100, 110, 120, 130) cm]

Using circular needle CO 104 (108, 108, 108, 108) sts. Do not join. Work back and forth in garter st. When piece measures 1″ [2.5 cm], add first buttonhole (RS): k 5, ssk, yo, work to end. Repeat the buttonhole row every 2″ [5 cm] for 4 more times (*note: only 3 buttonholes are worked on collar, continue working the buttonholes on yoke*). Continue in garter st until the collar measures 6″ [15 cm], ending with a RS row.

Yoke

Continue working in St st and the button band in garter st. Work buttonholes as established on collar, every 2″ [5 cm].

Place markers on first row (WS): k 12, p 11 (12, 12, 13, 14), pm, p 12 (12, 12, 10, 8), pm, p 34 (36, 36, 38, 40), pm, p 12 (12, 12, 10, 8), pm, p 11 (12, 12, 13, 14), k to end.

SHORT ROWS FOR NECK SHAPING

SHORT ROW 1 (RS): *k until 2 sts before marker remain, m1R, k2, sm, k2, m1L; repeat three more times from *, k1, turn your work.

SHORT ROW 2 (WS): yo, p to last marker, sm, p4, turn work.

SHORT ROW 3 (RS): yo, *k until 2 sts before marker remain, m1R, k2, sm, k2, m1L; repeat three more times from *, k to previous yo, k2tog the yo with the next st, turn work.

SHORT ROW 4 (WS): yo, p to previous yo, ssp the yo with the next st, turn work.

Repeat short rows 3 and 4 twice. Work to end of row on next row (RS): yo, *k until 2 sts before marker remain, m1R, k2, sm, k2, m1L; repeat three more times from *, k to previous yo, k2tog the yo with the next st, k to end. Next row on WS: k 12, p to last yo, ssp the yo with the next st, p until 12 sts remain, k to end.

Raglan increases

Row 5 (RS): *k until 2 sts before marker remain, m1R, k2, sm, k2, m1L; repeat three more times from *, k to end.

Row 6 (WS): k 12, p until 12 sts remain, k to end. Repeat rows 5 and 6—13 (16, 20, 23, 26) times more.

Divide for body and sleeves

(RS): *k to m, remove marker, place the sts before next m on holder for sleeve, remove m; repeat once from *, k to end.

You have now 50 (56, 64, 68, 72) sts on both holders for sleeves and 156 (172, 188, 204, 220) sts on the needle for the body.

Body

Continue even in St st, but work the last and first 12 sts in garter st for button band as established. After 3 rows, join in round as follows (RS):

Place the last 12 sts on a dpn and hold the dpn parallel behind the left end of the working circular needle. Place marker for beginning of round and k2tog one stitch from each the circular needle and the dpn until all stitches from

dpn are worked up (12 sts decreased; 144 (160, 176, 192, 208) sts remain).

Continue working in the round in St st and work the first 12 sts of rnd in garter st for 8 rounds. Work even in St st until the body measures 11″ [27 cm] from underarm.

Add a garter st patch to the front as follows: work in St st until 12 sts remain, work to end in garter st. Continue as established until the body measures 14″ [35 cm] from underarm. Work additional 3″ [8 cm] in garter st, but work the first st of rnd in St st. BO sts loosely.

Sleeves

Note: You can pick up a few extra sts from the underarm to prevent a hole (decrease these sts on next possible round) — or you can sew the hole when finishing the garment. When working each sleeve as written, the garter st patch will be on different part of the sleeve. That is an intentional detail of the sweater.

Place the 50 (56, 64, 68, 72) sts of sleeve from holder on dpns. Join yarn and pm to indicate beginning of the round. Work even in St st until the sleeve measures 13″ [34 cm] from underarm.

Add a garter st patch to the sleeve as follows: work in St st until 12 sts remain, work to end in garter st. Continue as established until the sleeve measures 16″ [41 cm] from underarm. Work additional 3″ [8 cm] in garter st, but work the first st of rnd in St st. BO sts loosely.

Finishing

Weave in all yarn ends and sew on buttons. Wet block the pullover to measurements.

Grid Plan

Round and round you go; add some texture and the Grid Plan is ready! A wonderful deep brown color makes this extra soft cowl even more wonderful to wear, and with big needles it knits up super quick.

Materials

Yarn

2 skeins of Primo Aran by The Plucky Knitter (75% merino, 25% cashmere, 5% nylon; 200 yds [182 m] per 100 g). Approx. 400 yards [364 meters] of aran weight yarn. Sample was knit in the colorway "Chocolate Crinkle."

Needles

US 10 [6 mm] circular needles; 32″ [80 cm] long. Adjust needle size if necessary to obtain the correct gauge.

Notions

A stitch marker, tapestry needle, blocking aids.

Sizing

One size

Finished measurements: 48″ [122 cm] in circumference and 12″ [30 cm] deep.

Gauge

15 sts and 24 rows = 4″ [10 cm] in Stockinette stitch.

Chart A

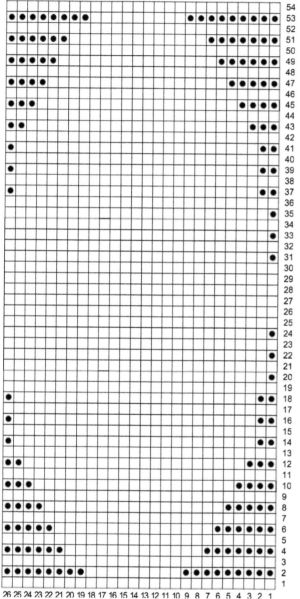

NOTE: READ THE CHART FROM RIGHT TO LEFT ON EACH
ROUND.

Loop cowl

Using circular needle, CO 182 sts. Join in round, carefully not twisting your stitches. Pm for beginning of round and work in garter st (alternate k and p rounds) until the piece measures 1½" [4 cm]. End with a purl round. Continue working through all rows of Chart A – you will have 7 chart repeats in one round. Change to garter st after all chart rows and work additional 1½" [4 cm]. BO sts loosely.

Finishing

Weave in all yarn ends. Block the cowl to measurements using your preferred method.

Be Mine

Be Mine is a cardigan you can wear across the seasons. A lovely loose funnel neck, short row shaping at the neck and A-line shaping in the body make this cardigan fun to knit and easy to wear.

Materials

Yarn

3 (3, 3, 4, 4, 4) skeins of Top Draw Socks by Skein (85% merino, 15% nylon; 437 yds [400 m] per skein). Approx. 1050 (1160, 1340, 1460, 1580, 1700) yards [960 (1060, 1220, 1340, 1440, 1560) meters] of fingering weight yarn. Sample was knit in the colorway "Be Mine" and in size small.

Needles

US 2½ [3 mm] and US 4 [3.5 mm] circular needles, 32" [80 cm] long, and dpns. Adjust needle size if necessary to obtain the correct gauge.

Notions

Six 1" [2.5 cm] buttons, tapestry needle, stitch markers, stitch holders/waste yarn and blocking aids.

Sizing

XS (S, M, L, XL, XXL)

Finished chest circumference: 32 (36, 40, 44, 48, 52)" [80 (90, 100, 110, 120, 130) cm]. Choose a size with no ease to a small amount of positive ease.

Gauge

22 sts and 36 rows = 4" [10 cm] in Stockinette stitch using larger needle.

Finished Measurements

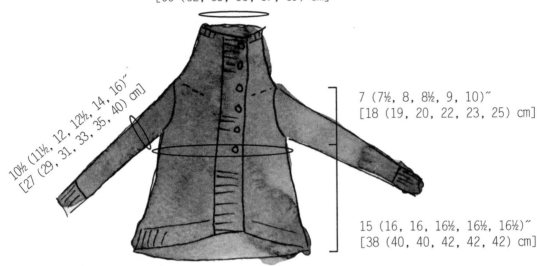

24 (25, 25½, 26, 27, 27½)″
[60 (62, 63, 65, 67, 69) cm]

10½ (11½, 12, 12½, 14, 16)″
[27 (29, 31, 33, 35, 40) cm]

7 (7½, 8, 8½, 9, 10)″
[18 (19, 20, 22, 23, 25) cm]

15 (16, 16, 16½, 16½, 16½)″
[38 (40, 40, 42, 42, 42) cm]

32 (36, 40, 44, 48, 52)″
[80 (90, 100, 110, 120, 130) cm]

Collar

Using smaller circ needle, CO 110 (114, 118, 122, 126, 130) sts. Do not join. Work 4 rows back and forth in St st. Continue in 1×1 ribbing until piece measures 1¼″ [3 cm]. Change to larger circ needle and work in St st. Place markers for increases on next row (RS): k 22 (23, 24, 25, 26, 27), pm, k 66 (68, 70, 72, 74, 76), pm, k to end.

Increase 5 (7, 8, 12, 14, 16) times on every 6th (6th, 6th, 4th, 4th, 4th) row (RS): *k until one st before m remain, m1R, k1, sm, k1, m1L; repeat once from *, k to end. Work 5 more rows in Stockinette stitch after last increase row.

Yoke

Continue in St st working sleeve cap increases and short rows for neck shaping. *Note: first you work short rows around right shoulder, then around left shoulder.*

Setup short row 1 (RS): k until one st before m remain, pm, m1L, k1, remove m, k1, m1R, pm, k8, turn work.

Setup short row 2 (WS): yo, p until 1 st before m remain, slip the next st, sm, m1R, p to m, m1L, sm, slip the next st, p8, turn work.

SHORT ROW 3 (RS): yo, k until one st before m remain, sm, m1L, k to m, m1R, sm, k to previous yo, k2tog the yo with the next st, turn work.

SHORT ROW 4 (WS): yo, p until 1 st before m remain, slip the next st, sm, m1R, p to m, m1L, sm, slip the next st, p to previous yo, ssp the yo with the next st, turn work.

Repeat short rows 3 and 4 — 4 times more.

Work to left shoulder on next row—

SETUP SHORT ROW 5 (RS): yo, k until one st before m remain, sm, m1L, k to m, m1R, sm, k to previous yo, k2tog the yo with the next st, k until one st before m remain, pm, m1L, k1, remove m, k1, m1R, pm, k8, turn work.

SETUP SHORT ROW 6 (WS): yo, p until 1 st before m remain, slip the next st, sm, m1R, p to m, m1L, sm, slip the next st, p8, turn work.

SHORT ROW 7 (RS): yo, k until one st before m remain, sm, m1L, k to m, m1R, sm, k to previous yo, k2tog the yo with the next st, turn work.

SHORT ROW 8 (WS): yo, p until 1 st before m remain, slip the next st, sm, m1R, p to m, m1L, sm, slip the next st, p to previous yo, ssp the yo with the next st, turn work.

Repeat short rows 7 and 8 — 4 times more.

Continue working to front with next set of short rows —

SHORT ROW 9 (RS): yo, k until one st before m remain, sm, m1L, k to m, m1R, sm, k to previous yo, k2tog the yo with the next st, turn work.

SHORT ROW 10 (WS): yo, *p until 1 st before m remain, slip the next st, sm, m1R, p to m, m1L, sm, slip the next st, p to previous yo, ssp the yo with the next st; repeat once from *, turn work.

SHORT ROW 11 (RS): yo, *k until one st before m remain, sm, m1L, k to m, m1R, sm; repeat once from *, k to previous yo, k2tog the yo with the next st, turn work.

SHORT ROW 12 (WS): yo, *p until 1 st before m remain, slip the next st, sm, m1R, p to m, m1L, sm, slip the next st, p to previous yo, ssp the yo with the next st; repeat once from *, turn work.

Repeat short rows 11 and 12 until you have 50 (50, 50, 50, 52, 56) sts for each sleeve (between markers). Work whole rows in St st and slip the sts next to markers as established. On first rows pick up the last two yarn-overs – k2tog the yo with the next st on RS and ssp the you together with next st on WS. Continue even in St st and slipped seam sts until the armhole measures 7 (7, 7, 7¼, 7¾, 8)" [17 (17, 17, 18, 19, 20) cm] – *note: measure from the slipped stitch seam.*

INCREASE FOR UNDERARMS (RS): *k until 3 sts before m remain, m1R, k3, sm, k2, m1L, k until 2 sts before m remain, m1R, k2, sm, k3, m1L; repeat once from *, k to end.

Repeat the increase row 2 (3, 4, 5, 6, 7) more times on every RS row.

DIVIDE FOR BODY AND SLEEVES

*K to m, remove m, place all sts before next m on holder for sleeve, CO 0 (2, 3, 4, 5, 8) using backward-loop cast-on, pm, CO another 0 (2, 3, 4, 5, 8) using backward-

loop cast-on, remove m; repeat once from *, k to end.

You have now 58 (60, 62, 64, 68, 72) sts on each holder for the sleeves and 142 (166, 186, 210, 230, 254) sts on the needle for the body.

Body

Continue in St st. When the body measures 2 (2, 2, 3, 3, 3)″ [5 (5, 5, 8, 8, 8) cm] from underarm, begin increases working the increase row every 4th row (RS): *k until 4 sts before m remain, m1L, k to m, sm, k4, m1R, repeat once from *, k to end.

After two increase rows start short rows and continue increases as established —

Setup short row 13 (RS): k to m, sm, k to m, sm, k10, turn work.

Setup short row 14 (WS): yo, p to m, sm, p to m, sm, p10, turn work.

Short row 15 (RS): yo, k to m and work increase on every second time, sm, k to m and work increases on every second time, sm, k to previous yo working increase every second time, k2tog the yo with the next st, k3, turn work.

Short row 16 (WS): yo, p to m, sm, p to m, sm, p to previous yo, ssp the yo with the next st, p3, turn work.

Work short rows 15 and 16 five more times. Work whole rows in St st for additional 1″ [2.5 cm] and increase as established. On first two whole rows pick up the last two yarn-overs – k2tog the yo with the next st on RS and ssp the you together with next st on WS.

Repeat the short row set once more, beginning with

short row 13 and ending with 1″ [2.5 cm] of St st. Work even in St st until the body measures 12 (13, 13, 13½, 13½, 13½)″ [30 (32, 32, 34, 34, 34) cm] from underarm. Change to smaller circ needle and work 3″ [8 cm] in 1×1 ribbing. BO sts loosely in ribbing.

Sleeves

Note: You can pick a few extra stitches from the underarm for all sizes to prevent hole – or sew the gap while finishing the garment. Decrease these extra picked up stitches on next possible round. Do not decrease the additional sts CO for underarm.

Place the 58 (60, 62, 64, 68, 72) sts of sleeve from holder on larger dpns. Pick up and knit 0 (2, 3, 4, 5, 8) sts from left side of the CO edge of underarm, k to end, pick up and knit 0 (2, 3, 4, 5, 8) sts from right side of the CO edge of underarm and pm to indicate middle of the round. You have 58 (64, 68, 72, 78, 88) sts on needles. Work even in St st until the sleeve measures 4″ [10 cm] from underarm.

DECREASE ROUND: k2, ssk, k until 4 sts remain, k2tog, k to end.

Repeat the decrease round 4 times more every 2″ [5 cm] – 48 (54, 58, 62, 68, 78) sts remain. Work even St st until sleeve measures 16″ [40 cm]. Change to smaller dpns and work 4″ [10 cm] in 1×1 ribbing. BO sts loosely in ribbing.

Button Plackets

LEFT PLACKET

Using smaller circ needle and RS facing, pick up and knit 126 (132, 138, 146, 152, 160) sts. *Note: pick up stitches in ratio 2 stitches every 3 rows, especially if your row gauge differs significantly.*

Work in 1×1 ribbing until the button placket measures 3¾″ [9 cm]. Work in St st until the placket is 4″ [10 cm] deep. BO sts loosely.

RIGHT PLACKET

Using smaller circ needle and RS facing, pick up and knit 126 (132, 138, 146, 152, 160) sts. *Note: pick up stitches in ratio 2 stitches every 3 rows, especially if your row gauge differs significantly.*

Work in 1×1 ribbing until the button placket measures 2¾″ [7 cm].

Work buttonholes on **right placket only** (RS): work in ribbing until 13 (13, 13, 16, 16, 16)″ [33 (33, 33, 40, 40, 40) cm] of the placket stitches remain, ending with a knit st, *yo, k2tog, work 2 (2, 2, 2¼, 2¼, 2¼)″ [5 (5, 5, 6, 6, 6) cm] in ribbing; repeat five times from *, yo, k2tog, work to end in ribbing.

Continue in 1×1 ribbing until the button placket measures 3¾″ [9 cm]. Work in St st until the placket is 4″ [10 cm] deep. BO sts loosely.

Finishing

Weave in all yarn ends. Sew on buttons to left placket. Block cardigan to measurements using preferred method.

Cable Scarf

A LOVELY CABLED TEXTURE AND COMPLETELY REVERSIBLE DESIGN — WHAT MORE COULD YOU NEED FROM A SCARF? THIS PIECE IS WORKED IN RICH MERINO WOOL FOR EXTRA WARMTH.

Materials

Yarn

3 skeins of Merino DK by String Theory (100% superwash merino; 280 yds [256 m] per skein). Approx. 680 yards [615 meters] of DK to worsted weight yarn. Sample was knit in the colorway Carina.

Needles

US 6 [4 mm] circular needles or straight needles. Adjust needle size if necessary to obtain the correct gauge.

Notions

Cable needle, tapestry needle, blocking aids.

Sizing

One size

Finished measurements: 71″ [180 cm] long and 10″ [25 cm] wide.

Gauge

26 sts and 28 rows = 4″ [10 cm] in 1×1 ribbing, un-stretched.

Stitch Patterns

TWISTED RIBBING

*k1 tbl, p1; repeat from * to end on RS and *k1, p1 tbl; repeat from * to end on WS.

1×1 RIBBING

*k1, p1; repeat from * to end.

C8B (RIBBING)

Slip 4 sts on cable needle and hold at back of the work, work the next 4 sts in ribbing, work the 4 sts from cable needle in ribbing.

C8F (RIBBING)

Slip 4 sts on cable needle and hold at front of the work, work the next 4 sts in ribbing, work the 4 sts from cable needle in ribbing.

Instructions

CO 64 sts. Work back and forth in 1×1 twisted ribbing until the ribbing measures 1″ [2.5 cm]. Change to normal 1×1 ribbing and cables as follows:

ROWS 1-8 AND 10: work in 1×1 ribbing

ROW 9, CABLE ROW A: work 8 sts in 1×1 ribbing, C8B (ribbing), work 16 sts in ribbing, C8F (rib-bing), work 8 sts in ribbing, C8F (ribbing, work to end in ribbing.

Work rows 1-10 two more times.

ROWS 11-18 AND 20: work in 1×1 ribbing.

ROW 19, CABLE ROW B: C8F (ribbing), work 8 sts in 1×1 ribbing, C8F (ribbing), C8B (ribbing), work 8 sts in ribbing, C8B (ribbing), work 8 sts in ribbing, C8B (ribbing).

Work rows 11-20 four more times.

Continue cable patterning as follows: work rows 1-10 five times, work rows 11-20 nine times, work rows 1-10 five times, work rows 11-20 nine times, work rows 1-10 three times. End the scarf with 1″ [2.5 cm] of twisted ribbing. BO sts loosely in ribbing.

Finishing

Weave in all yarn ends. Block the scarf to measurements using your preferred method.

Beetle Cap

THE BEETLE CAP IS WORKED IN A TEXTURED HERRINGBONE STITCH FOR EXTRA WARMTH, AND THE VISOR MAKES IT LOOK BOTH CHIC AND FUN. THIS PIECE IS WORKED FROM THE BRIM UP AND THE VISOR IS WORKED LAST.

Materials

YARN

1 skein of Merino Sport by The Uncommon Thread (100% superwash merino; 285 yds [262 m] per 100 g). Approx. 200 (260 285) yards [meters] of sport weight yarn. Sample was knit in the colorway Plata and in kid's size.

NEEDLES

US 2½ [3 mm] and US 10 [6 mm] dpns. Adjust needle size if necessary to obtain the correct gauge.

NOTIONS

Stitch markers, tapestry needle, pins, blocking aids.

Sizing

KIDS (WOMEN, MEN)

Brim circumference: 16½ (18, 20)˝ [42 (46, 50) cm] unstretched.

Gauge

20 sts and 24 rows = 4˝ [10 cm] in herringbone stitch pattern using larger needle

22 sts and 28 rows = 4˝ [10 cm] Stockinette stitch using smaller needle.

Stitch Patterns

HERRINGBONE PATTERN (IN THE ROUND)

ROUND 1: k2tog slipping the first st off the needle, *k2tog the remaining st with the next st, slip only the first st off the needle; repeat from * to end of rnd.

ROUND 2: k2tog tbl slipping the first st off the left needle, *k2tog tbl the remaining st with the next st, slip only the first st off the needle; repeat from * to end of rnd.

Note: When you come to beginning of the round marker (one st remaining), remove m and work the last and first st as on previous rnd (k2tog or k2tog tbl), slip first st off the needle and pm for beg of rnd.

Brim and body

Using smaller dpns, CO 90 (102, 110) sts. Join in round, carefully not twisting your stitches. Pm for beg of rnd and work 6 rounds in St st. Change to larger dpns and continue in herringbone stitch. Work until the cap measures 6½ (8, 9)″ [17 (20, 23) cm] from brim. Decrease on next round 1 as follows: k2tog all the way to end of round. Repeat the decrease round on every 6th round two more times working the regular rounds in herringbone pattern as established. Cut yarn and thread through the remaining sts after last decrease round.

Visor

Measure and mark with pins 5½ (6, 6½)″ [14 (15, 16) cm] from the middle of the front to each side to make sure your visor is right in the middle of the cap. Using smaller dpns, pick up and knit 60 (66, 72) sts from the front brim. Pick up from beginning of herringbone pattern, RS facing.

Work in garter st and start short rows – *note: do not pick up wraps; they will blend in garter st nicely.*

SETUP SHORT ROW (WS): Knit until 15 (17, 19) remain, pm, W&T.

SETUP SHORT ROW (RS): m1R, sm, k until 15 (17, 19) sts remain, pm, m1L, W&T.

SHORT ROW 1 (WS): K until you've worked the previous wrapped st, W&T.

SHORT ROW 2 (RS): K to m, m1R, sm, k to m, sm, m1L, K until you've worked the previous wrapped st, W&T.

Continue working one more st after each W&T and increasing on each RS row until you've wrapped the first and last st of row. Work to end on next row. BO sts loosely.

Finishing

Weave in all yarn ends. Block the cap to measurements using your preferred method.

Techniques

Techniques

THREE-NEEDLE BIND-OFF

Divide those stitches you are going to join, evenly on two separate needles. Hold the needles parallel and using a third needle, k2tog first stitch on each needle. *Knit the next stitch on each needle together similarly and pass the previous knitted stitch over the next and off the needle; repeat from * until all stitches are worked.

SHORT ROWS WITH WRAP AND TURN (W&T)

Work to the point where pattern says W&T. Bring your yarn to the front of the work, slip the next st from the left hand needle, take your yarn to the back of the work, slip the st back to the left hand needle. Turn your work. Do not pick up wraps later.

SHORT ROWS WITH YARN-OVER

Work to the point where pattern says *turn work*. Work a yarn-over right after turning. The yarn-over will be worked together with the next stitch, next time this place of the piece is worked.

GRAFTING

Kitchener Stitch. Arrange the stitches you are going to join on two needles so that you have the same number of stitches on each needle. Hold the needles parallel with WS of the work together. Thread working yarn on a tapestry needle. Bring yarn through the first stitch on the needle at front as if to purl leaving st on needle, bring needle through the first st on the needle at the back as if to knit leaving st on needle. *Bring needle through the first st of front needle as if to knit and slip st off needle, bring needle through the next st of front needle as if to purl leaving st on needle, bring needle through the first st of back needle as if to purl and slip st off needle, bring needle through the next st of back needle as if to knit leaving st on needle; repeat from * until 1 st remains on each needle. To finish, bring needle through the last st of front needle as if to knit and slip st off needle, bring needle through the last st of back needle as if to purl and slip st off needle.

BACKWARD-LOOP CAST-ON

Make a loop with working yarn and place it on right needle backwards (the way it will stay on the needle) and tighten stitch.

Abbreviations

CO: cast on

BO: bind off

st(s): stitch(es)

k: knit

p: purl

rnd: round, rounds

RS: right side

WS: wrong side

MC: main color

CC: contrasting color

St st: Stockinette stitch; knit on RS and purl on WS.

rev St st: reversed Stockinette stitch; purl on RS and knit on WS.

garter st: garter stitch. In the round: alternate knit and purl rounds; back and forth: knit each row.

pm: place stitch marker

sm: slip marker

yo: yarn-over

k2tog: knit 2 sts together; decrease

k3tog: knit 3 sts together; decrease

p2tog: purl 2 sts together; decrease

p3tog: purl 2 sts together; decrease

ssk: slip, slip, knit slipped sts tbl; decrease.

sssk: slip, slip, slip, knit slipped sts tbl; decrease.

ssp: slip, slip, purl slipped sts tbl; decrease.

sssp: slip, slip, slip, purl slipped sts tbl; decrease.

m1R: right leaning increase, make one right; lift loop between stitches from the back, knit into the front of the loop.

m1L: left leaning increase, make one left; lift loop between stitches from the front, knit into the back of the loop.

m1R (purl): right leaning increase, make one right; lift loop between stitches from the back, purl into the front of the loop.

m1L (purl): left leaning increase, make one left; lift loop between stitches from the front, purl into the back of the loop.

kfb: knit into front and back of the same one stitch; increase.

Abbreviations

Find the lovely yarns in this book

HOPEASÄIE	etsy.com/shop/Hopeasaie
LIONESS ARTS	etsy.com/shop/LionessArts
LOUHITTAREN LUOLA	tuulia.blogspot.fi
MADELINETOSH	madelinetosh.com
MALABRIGO	malabrigoyarn.com
THE PLUCKY KNITTER	thepluckyknitter.com
RINTALAN LUOMUTILA	rintalantila.fi
SKEIN	skeinyarn.com
STRING THEORY	stringtheoryyarn.com
THE UNCOMMON THREAD	theuncommonthread.co.uk

Sources

Barber, E. J. W. (1991): *Prehistoric Textil*

Pekonen, O. et.al. (2003): *Elämän Värit*

Salmela, T. (2012): *Kehrääjän käsikirja*

Tetri, A-K. (2008): *Luonnonvärjäys*

coloria.net

The Finnish sources have been freely translated to English by the author.

Thank You

Jonna and Amanda.

Akshata.

All my wonderful models: Annukka, Sini, Alina,
Aurora, Timo, John, Aarni, Okko and Iisakki.

Maisa, Olli and Helmi.
Grandma and Grandpa.

Mum.

Sarah, Ce, Danielle and Amy – thank you for your
generosity and for creating so many amazing
colors. It's pure magic.

Patient and astonishing test knitters.
The whole knitting community and all the
wonderful dyers around the world!

Color Wheel Knits

ISBN 13 (print): 978-1-937513-67-2
First English language edition published by Cooperative Press
http://www.cooperativepress.com

Translated by the author from her book *Lankaleikki: Neuleita käsinvärjätyistä*, first published in Finnish by Atena

Patterns © 2015 Veera Välimäki
Text © 2015 Veera Välimäki

O. 12/15
H 6/16
B 12/16
W 6/17
O 12/17
H 6/18

CPSIA information can be obtained
at www.ICGtesting.com
Printed in the USA
LVOW05s0947071115
461528LV00018B/74/P